THE ABOLITION OF WOMAN

FIORELLA NASH

The Abolition of Woman

How Radical Feminism
Is Betraying Women

IGNATIUS PRESS   SAN FRANCISCO

Cover photo:
©istock/ianmcdonnell

Cover design by Riz Boncan Marsella

CONTENTS

ACKNOWLEDGEMENTS

There are many individuals I have to thank for assisting me on the journey to writing this book: Anthony McCarthy, who deserves a special mention for his endless encouragement and advice; John Smeaton and my colleagues at The Society for the Protection of Unborn Children (SPUC), for allowing me the time and space to write the book and for sharing their expertise on the many complex moral issues I have attempted to cover. Without the support of SPUC and the opportunity to develop these ideas on the lecture circuit, this book could never have been written.

I must also thank my husband, Edmund, for proving that there is no contradiction between chivalry and the support of a wife's career. I should also mention the hostile voices from both ends of the political spectrum who have unwittingly strengthened my resolve to explore what pro-life feminism really means for women in the twenty-first century.

I owe the greatest debt of gratitude, however, to author, historian and prolific letter writer Ann Farmer, who first suggested to me long ago that pro-life feminism is possible. I still have in my possession the book she sent me in response to a sarcasm-laden denunciation of feminism I penned as an angry student. The book contained no accompanying letter, just a Post-It note on the front cover containing the words "Pro-life Feminism *does* exist!"

Sometimes, the most life-changing messages are the shortest.

INTRODUCTION

Like many women of my generation, I like to imagine that I would have been a suffragette if I had been living over a hundred years ago, though I might have drawn the line at setting fire to post boxes, destroying valuable artworks and throwing myself in front of a horse. Everyone loves a rebel, though usually not when he is in the process of rebelling.

As a child of the 1980s, there were certain things I took for granted. Britain had its first female prime minister in the person of Margaret Thatcher; I accepted that a woman could get more or less where she wanted in life if she worked hard and had a forceful enough personality. My own mother worked full-time alongside my father. However, coming from an immigrant family with a very different cultural perspective on womanhood, I also learnt very young (and with an increasing sense of frustration) that being a female carried certain restrictions with it that I was expected to accept. I have never forgotten the shocked silence I managed to cause in my early teens when my male cousin clicked his fingers during dinner and demanded I fetch him a glass of water, only to receive the response from me, "Get it yourself! You have a pair of legs, haven't you?"

It was drummed into us from the earliest moments that there was only one virtue a girl could aspire to and that was obedience in all things; the slightest hint of a strong will in a girl was treated as dangerous and in need of swift discipline. Every detail of our lives was controlled, down to the way we wore our hair to the way we walked (to this day, I still do not quite understand why the length of my stride can be condemned as unladylike). While other girls were embracing life as they seemed to want to live it, I was trapped in a world that thwarted girls at every step and was stubbornly refusing to reform.

My 1990s English convent school education introduced me to feminism for the first time, but far from providing a young woman with the tools to develop intellectually, the feminism of the baby boomer generation came across as laughably antiquated, petty and self-pitying. Whilst women in some parts of the world were struggling with the spectre of honour killings and child marriage, female members of staff railed against any use of the word "man" in the liturgy and talked about men as though they had nothing better to do than concoct wicked plots against female emancipation. Our senior boarding mistress, who was Catholic and female but clearly resented being both, epitomised what I imagined to be the worst excesses of radical feminism— marriage was a lonely and depressing existence for women, the Catholic priesthood included fear of women as part of the job description and the Church had personally prohibited her daughter from being an altar server because she didn't have a penis.

At university and in the years that followed, the guardians of women's rights vacillated between victimhood and thuggery, with doses of racism and neo-colonialism thrown into the mix. Women who claimed to stand for all of us were quick to assume their cultural superiority without always realising that they were imposing a white, Western, middle-class agenda on an increasingly diverse and international female student body. The young woman who proposed that the Women's Union disaffiliate from the National Abortion Campaign had her right to express a considered opinion encouraged by a student woman's officer who scowled, shouted and shook her fist in her face. Abortion, of course, was the untouchable jewel in the crown of women's liberation.

Feminism, or so it appeared, was as prescriptive and tyrannical as the status quo of the past had ever been. Women were still expected to conform to a narrow set of maxims, and "real" womanhood was still being defined for women with an expectation of conformity at the risk of social opprobrium. To be a proper woman, one had to be single but probably sexually active, antireligion, anti-marriage, antimotherhood, antimen, pro-abortion and pro-contraception. Any woman who expressed the right to choose their own way was a self-hating antifeminist deviant who needed bullying and shaming back into the fold or silencing altogether.

That women still faced struggles, I had no doubt, but if feminism had become so trapped in the battles of the past, so dictatorial, so obsessed with its own victimhood, it was no longer fit for purpose. As far as I was concerned, a woman caught between two conflicting and unsatisfactory ideologies of womanhood would simply have to fight her corner her way. Not long after I had rather publicly said so, the parcel arrived on my doorstep from a well-wisher, containing a slim volume of essays by women who were feminist but rejected the ideology of abortion: *Swimming against the Tide.*[1] Pro-life feminism did exist, I was assured. It was simply a case of finding it.

My initial reaction to the discovery that there were pro-life feminist groups that had been in existence for decades,

---

[1] Angela Kennedy, ed., *Swimming against the Tide* (Dublin, Ireland: Four Courts Press, 1997).

was relief that pro-life women had a "safe place" to go intellectually, and the capacity to fight for equality without being forced to go against their own consciences. The ongoing struggle for equality needs the contribution of pro-life feminism if the complex challenges and difficulties facing women in the twenty-first century are to be adequately met; there is no such thing as an intellectual safe space, nor should there be.

Abortion has become virtually de fide within feminist discourse, an irrefutable doctrine that defines both what it means to be feminist and what it means to be female. There is some disagreement over whether Florynce Kennedy, Gloria Steinem or an elderly Irishwoman in a taxi came up with the notorious claim: "If men could get pregnant, abortion would be a sacrament." Repugnant though it is, there is perhaps no better place to begin an exploration into the abolition of woman than with this statement. Everything about it says a great deal more about the thinking that produced such an assertion than about abortion itself: women are hard-done-by and misunderstood—only a woman can have an abortion, which is therefore why abortion tends to be viewed negatively; the Church specifically fails to celebrate abortion because it involves women not men (the word "sacrament" being a deliberate act of spiritual appropriation here with its allusion to Catholic and Orthodox theology); abortion is as central to women's liberation and as much a blessing to women as the sacraments are to the souls of the faithful. In the minds of Kennedy or Steinem or those whose words they have used, abortion is accepted unquestioningly as an act of salvation.

It is in the nature of social movements to become part of the establishment, and in some respects it is a mark of success when a movement's leaders make the transition from rebels to authority figures, but if a dissident movement becomes part of a corrupt establishment, assuming the same tyrannical behaviour it was founded to fight, then other dissidents must inevitably rise to challenge the new orthodoxy. In that sense, my book is one of dissent. However, in exploring the inherently misogynistic principles and practices underlying abortion to which contemporary feminism has become wilfully blind, it is my hope that it will also provide a positive way forward for women who may previously have seen the terms "pro-life" and "feminist" as diametrically opposed.

This book started life as a series of lectures aimed at university students and has developed in part as a result of the passionate but always informative discussions and feedback I have received when speaking on this most sensitive of subjects. For this reason, the book is best read as a number of interconnected essays which collectively put the case for a pro-life feminist approach to all the major beginning-of-life issues, including abortion, surrogacy, IVF and maternal health in developing countries, but which also explores the realities of pregnancy, motherhood and infertility for women. Through the book, I seek to expose the calculated way in which contemporary feminists have silenced dissent within their own ranks on the subject of abortion, demonised and alienated pro-life dissent and allowed abortion to be used as a weapon against women, through state population-control programmes, sex-selective abortion and the denial of full information about abortion.

In the name of liberating women and giving women back control of their own lives, the fetishisation of abortion and the dogmatic determination to ensure that all women speak with one voice in its defence, has created a new patriarchy which pits women against their own children, which pits women against other women. Pro-life feminism is not and cannot be a safe space for pro-life women to hide away from the tumult of feminist discourse or the battle for true equality between the sexes. Nor can it remain part of the pro-life movement's maverick fringe, indulged by mainstream pro-life campaigners because it defies the stereotypes and confuses the opposition. In the chapters that follow, I do not wish simply to argue that pro-life feminism is something other than a contradiction in terms, but that pro-life feminism should be a powerful movement at the forefront of the battle to defend the youngest and the most vulnerable human lives. The alternative is the abolition of woman.

The New Patriarchy and Its Dissenters

A Life Worth Sacrificing? Scientific Reality and the Right to Kill

It is possible to give "human being" a precise meaning. We can use it as equivalent to "member of the species Homo sapiens." Whether a being is a member of a given species is something that can be determined scientifically, by an examination of the nature of the chromosomes in the cells of living organisms. In this sense there is no doubt that from the first moments of its existence an embryo conceived from human sperm and egg is a human being.

—Peter Singer, *Practical Ethics*

Prior to the development of ultrasound and other medical advances such as in utero surgery, much of the debate surrounding the morality of abortion concerned prenatal development and the point at which life could be said to begin. Pro-life campaigners have fought hard to prove definitively that life begins at conception, whereas supporters of abortion have placed the beginnings of life later, such as at the appearance of the "primitive streak" (around fourteen days), the completion of organogenesis, "quickening" and so on.

However, as medical knowledge of prenatal development has become more sophisticated, the boundaries of the debate have begun to shift in directions that could

Peter Singer, *Practical Ethics*, 2nd ed. (Cambridge: Cambridge University Press, 1993), pp. 85–86.

not have been predicted when campaigns for abortion law reform began in earnest during the 1960s, and this shift continues to have serious implications both for pro-abortion arguments and pro-life responses.

Out and out denial of the humanity of the unborn continues despite the now routine use of ultrasound, including clear 4D ultrasound images and the growing body of evidence which demonstrates the ability of the unborn child to detect and respond to touch, sound, light and pain. Denial has always been a necessary defence mechanism for abortion advocates, but rather than have the courage to face scientific realities head-on, many supporters of abortion hide behind ever more elaborate and misleading language to conceal the truth of what abortion involves.

Descriptions of the unborn commonly used by abortion practitioners and campaigners include such imaginative expressions as "products of conception", "contents of the uterus", "pregnancy tissue", "foetal tissue" or indeed "parasite", "hijacker" and "invader". It is telling that after nearly fifty years of legal and widely available abortion in Britain, there remains a sharp dichotomy between the way abortionists describe unborn children and the way the rest of society describe them, a dichotomy that has yet to be convincingly explained by those who persist in using such dehumanising language. It is revealing that when the abortion industry's trade in fetal body parts was exposed to the world through a series of undercover videos, Planned Parenthood's Cecile Richards continued to refer to "our involvement with fetal tissue research" when members of her own organization had been caught on camera candidly discussing the value of baby livers and eyeballs.[1]

---

[1] Ryan Teague Beckwith, "Planned Parenthood Head Defends Fetal Tissue Research before Congress", *Time*, updated 29 September 2015, http://time.com/4053715/planned-parenthood-video-cecile-richards-congress/.

The need to deny the objective humanity of the unborn can result in some bizarre lapses in rational thinking, as a report on an ethics masterclass, published in British journal *Obs and Gynae News*, demonstrates.[2] The report begins by creating a straw man argument against "reductionism" which sees pregnancy in terms of two extremes—total focus on the rights of the woman or total focus on the rights of the baby. It is a common rhetorical tactic to manufacture extreme arguments so as to appear to occupy the middle ground of a debate, but the two extremes expressed in the report are based upon a caricature of the abortion debate. Arguments which completely ignore the rights of the unborn are a requisite of pro-abortion rhetoric (for all the talk about the "special status" of unborn babies/ embryos/fetuses, it is impossible to speak of respecting the rights of a human life one chooses to kill). By contrast, a truly consistent pro-life ethic respects the right to life of all members of the human family, and therefore the health and rights of the pregnant woman are as important as the life of the unborn child. There is no reductionism at the heart of such a position.

However, it is the approach to foetal rights taken by the report that is so problematic:

> To the pregnant woman, we have both autonomy-based and beneficence-based obligations. We also have beneficence-based obligations to the fetus when there are linkages between the fetus and the child the fetus will become. One such linkage is viability. Another such linkage occurs when the pregnant women confers on her pre-viable fetus the moral status of being a patient, based on

[2] Frank A. Chervenak, "A Sound Model of Obstetric Ethics", *Ob.Gyn .News*, 25 May 2012, http://www.obgynnews.com/views/master-class/blog view120622/a-sound-model-of-obstetric-ethics/2eec9c7349c2e7603e200dd35 7a36f63.html.

her beliefs and values. . . . The view that the fetus has rights,
such as an unconditional "right" to life, does not consider
the fact that there are irreconcilable differences among and
within the major religions of the world—and among cultures, philosophers, and other authoritative sources—on
the status of a pre-viable fetus and on fetal rights.[3]

The rights of human beings at different stages of their lives
and of particular racial and socio-economic groups have
been disputed—with disastrous consequences—on many
occasions in recent history, but human rights have never
been trophies to be handed out by others to those who
are deemed worthy of them. The Universal Declaration of
Human Rights at no point claims that any human right is
conditional upon the feelings of others.

What the report also fails to note is that the status of
women and born children varies according to cultural,
philosophical and religious traditions, but doctors would
be regarded as failing in their duty of care if they refrained
from protecting a patient's rights on any such grounds.
To give an example, a pregnant woman is admitted to
hospital suffering minor complications. As the midwife is
in the process of examining her, she notices bruising on
the woman's arm. For the sake of argument, let us say
that the bruising is entirely innocent, the result of iron
injections or a clumsily administered blood test, but the
midwife immediately suspects foul play. The appropriate course of action would be to question the pregnant
woman about the bruising and to offer help should the
woman report domestic abuse. What the midwife would
be highly unlikely to do would be to ignore the woman
altogether, turn to her husband and ask him what status his

[3] Ibid.

wife had in his culture. Did his belief system sanction wife beating? The philosophy of the husband and the moral status he wished to confer upon his wife would be an irrelevance, and the hospital concerned would take a very dim view of any medical professional who thought otherwise.

The notion that the unborn should be treated alternately as a baby or a mass of tissue dependent entirely upon whether or not the pregnancy is wanted may be intended as a way of supporting a woman's bodily autonomy, but this unscientific shifting of language unwittingly reinforces a misogynistic stereotype of women as shallow and childish, whose whims and fancies need to be humoured regardless of the facts: She wants an abortion; therefore let us call it a fetus to spare her feelings. She wants the baby, well let's call it a baby then; she'll like that. No organism can be radically altered by desire alone—I may wish my pet cat to be a canary, but fur will not become feathers because I desire my cat to be something it is not. If a kindly bystander were to tell me, "If you think it's a canary, my dear, it's a canary," it would be proof that the bystander had either lost possession of his mental faculties or believed I had. It would not be empowering or convincing in the least.

In the case of abortion, the constant shifts in language are the result of deliberate denial, a desperation to be convinced that abortion is a mere medical procedure or at least to convince women of this and—in part—an internal battle on the part of the abortion industry to accommodate the truth without admitting it. For this reason, abortion facilities may offer respectfully to dispose of a woman's "foetal tissue" in case of late-term abortion (assuming they do woman this courtesy) when the idea is nonsensical from either side of the debate. If the product of an abortion is mere tissue, it no more requires respectful disposal than the product of a tonsillectomy. If it is more than tissue, such respect is rather misplaced under the circumstances.

These logical lapses quickly descend into dangerous relativistic judgements about human value when supporters of abortion are faced with the difficulty of denying the significance of the unborn whilst at the same time being forced to acknowledge its humanity, albeit grudgingly. Ann Furedi, director of UK abortion provider BPAS, encapsulates this moral confusion in an article defending the "right to choose" position:

> For me the question is not: "When does human life begin?", because I think we can accept the embryo is a human life of sorts. For me the question is: "When does human life really begin to matter?" And that is something which can be relative to the woman who is carrying it.[4]

The physician of the German poet Goethe is purported to have said—in what could almost be a response to Furedi's position: "The physician should and may do nothing else but preserve life. Whether it is valuable or not, that is none of his business. If he once permits such considerations to influence his actions, the doctor will become the most dangerous man in the state." It was never the purpose of feminism, or any other movement concerned with the promotion of human rights, to determine when (if ever) a human life matters enough to be allowed to live. The extent to which a human being "matters" is none of anybody's business, and to fail to notice the dangers involved in defending such a position (promoted ironically in the

---

[4] "Ann Furedi: A Woman's Right to Choose Is Also Her Right to Be Human", *Independent*, 17 November 2008, http://www.independent.co.uk /voices/commentators/ann-furedi-a-womans-right-to-choose-is-also-her -right-to-be-human-1021691.html.

name of defending women's humanity) is to fail to learn the lessons of history. The moment relativism creeps into our understanding of the value of human life, the moment it becomes necessary to defend the value of human life for reasons other than the inherent value of being *human* itself, it becomes all too easy to make judgements about the right to life of any human being. From an entirely utilitarian perspective, does a child with profound learning difficulties "really matter"? Does an elderly person in the advanced stages of dementia "really matter"? Does a new-born baby matter as much as a fifty-year-old professor on the cusp of a major scientific discovery?

Few would truly wish to live in the sort of society in which human life could only be granted full rights, including the right to life, if it could be proven through entirely subjective tests to "really matter", but this is precisely the society the logic of abortion has created. It is the society in which we all live.

Killing as a Right

I want the general public to know what the doctors know: That this is a person. This is a baby. This is not some kind of blob of tissue.

—Dr Anthony Levatino, former abortionist[5]

A disturbing shift in the abortion debate has been the candid admission by some campaigners that abortion does indeed involve a deliberate act of killing. When the 4D images of babies walking in the womb hit the headlines over a

---

[5] Quoted in Randy Alcorn, *Pro-Life Answers to Pro-Choice Questions* (Danvers, Mass.: Multnomah Books, Crown Publishing Group, 2009), p. 206.

decade ago, a spokesman for the London-based Society
for the Protection of Unborn Children was quoted in the
media welcoming any evidence that raised awareness of
the humanity of unborn children, to which campaigner
Ellie Lee responded: "What did he reckon pregnant
women who have abortions think they are carrying? A
frog? A baby pig? Pregnant women who have abortions
(and those of us who unreservedly support their right to
do so) do know that fetuses are human."[6]

More recently, a *Salon* blogger commented: "I would
put the life of a mother over the life of a fetus every single
time—even if I still need to acknowledge my conviction
that the fetus is indeed a life. A life worth sacrificing."[7]

On one level, the increasing candour with which abortionists describe their work is simply a necessary tactic in
the face of improved technology and the valiant attempts
pro-life campaigners have made in recent years to expose
the grisly realities of abortion. When a series of undercover videos were released exposing the abortion industry's involvement in the sale of aborted baby parts, the
abortion industry and its many friends in the media went
to great lengths to smear the videos as deceptively edited
or as outright hoaxes. However, the more circumspect
members of the industry tend to be more prepared to own
up to the violence of the abortion procedure. At a Planned
Parenthood workshop in Michigan in 2014 for abortion
practitioners, one abortionist surprised her audience by
responding to a question about grisly images with: "Actually that's my week ... some weeks—and that's what it

[6] Ellie Lee, "The Trouble with 'Smiling' Fetuses", Pro-Choice Forum, 13
September 2003, http://www.prochoiceforum.org.uk/ocr_ethical_iss_1.php.
[7] Mary Elizabeth Williams, "So What If Abortion Ends Life?", *Salon*, 23 January 2013, http://www.salon.com/2013/01/23/so_what_if_abortion_ends_life/.

looks like. Ignoring the fetus is a luxury of activists and advocates. If you're a provider, you can't ignore the fetus, right, because the fetus is your marker of how well—how good a job you did." She goes on: "I actually think we should be less about denying the reality of those images and more about acknowledging that, yeah, that's quite a truth. So, given that we actually see the fetus the same way, and given that we might actually both agree that there's violence in here, ask me why I come to work every day. Let's just give them all the violence, it's a person, it's killing. Let's just give them all that. And then the more compelling question is, 'So, why is this the most important thing I could do with my life?'"[8]

It is a very frightening position. There is a refreshing honesty to it in the midst of the ever more desperate denials of the majority of abortion campaigners, but from every other angle, it is deeply unsettling. The debate has come a long way from "It's just a bundle of cells" to "It's killing. It's killing a human life, but we unreservedly support the right to kill." Or as journalist Antonia Senior put it: "The nearly 200,000 aborted babies in the UK each year are the lesser evil, no matter how you define life, or death, for that matter. If you are willing to die for a cause, you must be prepared to kill for it, too."[9] At a time when pro-life campaigners are increasingly portrayed as a security threat, it is a little ironic to read the words of a member of Britain's chattering classes who apparently

---

[8] Jonathon van Maren, "Five Things Everybody Needs to Know about the Leaked Planned Parenthood Footage", LifeSiteNews.com, 11 November 2015, https://www.lifesitenews.com/opinion/five-things-you-need-to-know -from-the-leaked-planned-parenthood-footage.

[9] Antonia Senior, "Yes, Abortion Is Killing. But It Is the Lesser Evil", *Times*, last updated 30 June 2010, http://www.scribd.com/doc/33782505/Yes -Abortion-is-Killing.

cannot see a difference between martyrdom and terror-
ism. Such a statement raises the obvious question, "Antonia, if that is what you sincerely believe, would you be
prepared to kill pro-life campaigners who obstruct your
cause? Would you be prepared to kill doctors and midwives who refuse to support your cause?"

This is not the language of feminism, nor is it in any
sense the language of social justice. The argument that
the vulnerable can and should be sacrificed in an act of
undeniable violence for the sake of maintaining control,
is misogynist not feminine or feminist in any sense of the
word.[10] It involves the establishment of the most brutal of hierarchies, and that was something feminism was
intended to oppose.

The Silencing of Female Dissent

It is only relatively recently in Western political history
that women's groups adopted the idea of abortion as a
right, and they did so in the teeth of considerable opposition from within their own ranks.[11] However, within the
space of little over a generation, the belief that abortion
is solely about a woman's right to choose and should
therefore be viewed as a positive (or at least neutral) practice, has become a matter of dogma from which no true

[10] Celia Wolf-Devine, "Abortion and the 'Feminine Voice'", accessed 8
February 2017, http://celiawolfdevine.com/pdf/Abortion-and-the-Feminine
-Voice.pdf.

[11] For a detailed account of the hijacking of America's women's movement
see Sue Ellen Browder's book *Subverted: How I Helped the Sexual Revolution
Hijack the Women's Movement* (San Francisco: Ignatius Press, 2015). David
Albert Jones' book *The Soul of the Embryo* (New York; London: Continuum,
2003) provides a detailed historical study on beliefs about the unborn and its
status across the centuries.

feminist may dissent. Those who do have the courage to oppose or at least question the validity of the right-to-choose dogma have faced the unhappy choice of keeping a low profile or abandoning feminism altogether, and in doing so, abandoning their dreams of fighting for a better world for women.

In an era of soundbites and what may be termed "bumper sticker philosophy", the slogan "a woman's right to choose" and its most famous variant "my body, my life, my right to decide" are trotted out like mantras to silence every argument and to divert attention to the real issues at stake. In her book *Subverted*, Browder quotes Noam Chomsky's observation about the use of slogans as propaganda tools:

> You want to create a slogan that nobody's going to be against and everybody's going to be for. Nobody knows what it means because it doesn't mean anything. Its crucial value is that it diverts your attention from the question that *does* mean something: Do you support our policy? That's the one you're not allowed to talk about.[12]

The power of the propagandist slogan—as defined by Chomsky—is as much to be found in its ability to silence the resistant minority as in its ability to rally the masses. Just as a persistently repeated lie very quickly becomes a point of received wisdom, the reduction of a complex moral issue into an easily repeatable one-liner, does more to forward a cause than any number of essays and political tracts could ever do (in fairness to the pro-abortion side, the pro-life movement must guard against the same temptation). Pro-life feminism asks the obvious question others

---

[12] Noam Chomsky, *Media Control: The Spectacular Achievements of Propaganda*, 2nd. ed. (New York: Seven Stories Press, 2011), p. 26.

choose to ignore: The right to choose *what*? My right to decide *what*? For women to be truly free, we must be intellectually free, and that means challenging and breaking loose from decades of indoctrinating propaganda that stems from that generous, memorable and wholly meaningless slogan "a woman's right to choose".

It has always been the role of feminism to question the status quo, and it is only intellectually honest to continue to do so, even if the status quo was in part forged by feminism itself. More than that, it is necessary to question contemporary feminism's unwavering allegiance to abortion for the sake of women who regard abortion as a betrayal of women but have been denied the right to say so.

The Colonisation of the Intellect

Aung San Suu Kyi, the Burmese freedom fighter who spent many years under house arrest for her pro-democracy beliefs, once wrote with tragic irony in the context of recent events: "To oppress the opposition is to assault the very foundation of democracy."[13] In virtually any other context, the deliberate and systematic oppression of an individual or a group who express unpopular or controversial opinions would be regarded as undemocratic and unacceptable in a modern, liberal society. If feminism had succeeded as a force for change, the bullying and suppression of female voices would not occur in contemporary society at all, let alone in the hallowed halls of feminist discourse itself, where women should be entitled to a voice and to be heard with respect. Instead, women who refuse

---

[13] Aung San Suu Kyi, *Letters from Burma* (London, UK; Penguin, 2010), p. 166.

to accept the ideology of abortion are openly bullied, vilified or patronised in the name of their own liberation.

Whereas diversity of opinion tends to be valued within feminism in other areas, the philosophy of contemporary feminism is underwritten by the assumption that to be female is to be pro-abortion, with those who oppose abortion treated as regrettable aberrations who require enlightenment. As one commentator on the US elections warned: "This desire for ideological purity hurts the feminist movement as a whole, because it divides feminists and alienates potential allies, reducing the movement's ability to accomplish change. It also creates a culture where feminists focus on proving themselves to other feminists, rather than on the battle for women's rights."[14]

The bullying and vilification of women who refuse to accept this ideology of abortion is one of the scandals of contemporary feminism which goes against the very notion that women have a right to freedom of conscience, freedom of speech and freedom of expression. At a meeting some years ago of the National Association of Women's Organisations in London, held at Amnesty International's opulent headquarters, a feminist MEP (Member of the European Parliament) attacked a fellow parliamentarian, the "notorious" (and absent) Anna Zaborska, for being "a right-wing Catholic" who "doesn't believe that women have any reproductive rights" (i.e., she opposes abortion).[15] The bitchiness with which Zaborska's views were attacked, complete with mimickry of her intonation, facial

---

[14] Anne Butcher, "Conservative Women Can Be Feminists Too", PANAM POST, 16 September 2016, https://panampost.com/valerie-marsman/2015/09/16/conservative-women-can-be-feminists-too/.

[15] National Association of Women's Organisations Meeting, Amnesty International Headquarters, London, September 2008.

expressions and mannerisms, pandered to the most disgusting female stereotypes without anyone present apparently noticing. Other delegates bemoaned the existence of
"antiwomen women" who were clearly not on the side
of their own sex because they opposed an apparently non-
negotiable vision of sexuality.

The term "antiwoman woman" is as meaningless as
the other slogans so beloved of the abortion movement—
what precisely is meant by a woman being against *herself*?
To suggest that women must conform to a particular ideological view of themselves or be categorised as childishly
self-destructive is surely to take a patriarchal position on
women as shallow and infantile. Secondly, it is difficult
to see how being antiabortion can be equated with being
antiwoman unless abortion worship has reached such
heights of absurdity that abortion itself has become synonymous with womanhood.

The most extreme propagation of this lie is typified by
politician Babette Josephs, a Pennsylvania Democrat who
lambasted women who had the temerity to vote against
abortion: "They must believe that they are not capable of
making their own health care choices, but they are capable of voting on bills that control all of our behaviour."
Josephs continued, "I don't understand it.... I don't
believe they're really women.... I believe they're men
with breasts."[16] It is of course possible that America is
being controlled by a regiment of men with breasts, but
it is perhaps more likely that women may be capable of
coming to the conclusion that abortion is wrong, freely
and without coercion.

---

[16] Charles Thompson, "Pennsylvania Representative Asks If Female
Co-Sponsors of State Ultrasound Bill Are 'Men with Breasts'", PennLive,
26 March 2012, http://www.pennlive.com/midstate/index.ssf/2012/03
/pennsylvania_state_rep_babette.html.

A less outlandish (though no less unjust) tactic to discredit women who reject abortion is to suggest that they are anti*feminist* women or something more akin to a feminist heretic, deviating from established doctrine and therefore in need of shaming or excommunication. Members of Feminists for Life of America have been attacked for "masquerading as feminists" because they oppose abortion and embrace the vision of the early feminists in their campaigning work and publications. In Australia, the pro-life Women's Forum have been accused of "faking it". In the words of a columnist for the *Sunday Sun-Herald*:

> If WFA [Women's Forum Australia] wants the government and private sector to adopt policies on women no different to those advocated by the Pope and some evangelical Christians, that's their prerogative. But all those hearing their case should also be told about the backgrounds of WFA's directors and the sum-total of the organisation's agenda so they can decide for themselves whether dispassionate feminist analysis of what will liberate women, or blind obedience to faith, is the source of their views.[17]

In the black-and-white world of the abortion campaigner, women fall into two distinct camps: the dispassionately rational and the blindly obedient. The rightness of abortion is apparently so obvious that any woman who disapproves cannot possibly have reached that conclusion independently, having carefully weighed up the evidence. The argument goes that they must have been brainwashed, blinkered or threatened in some way by the patriarchal hegemony. The fact that spokeswomen for pro-life

---

[17] "Women's Forum Australia Is 'Faking It'", *Sunday Sun-Herald*, 28 December 2008, http://cannold.com/articles/article/womens-forum-australia-is-faking-it/.

feminist groups are hardly shrinking violets does little to dispel this comforting belief.

If attacking the intellectual freedom of pro-life women were not enough, some abortion advocates have gone as far as to attack the sex lives of the majority of women who never undergo an abortion. At an Abortion Rights meeting in London's Parliament in May 2012, a columnist for the *Guardian* was reported to have said, to much laughter and applause: "If you reach the end of your life without having had an abortion, you are either a man or you haven't been laid much."[18]

Remarks such as these are clearly intended to be flippant but reveal a great deal about how low the intellectual level of the debate has fallen when women who oppose the status quo are portrayed as inadequate sexual failures for acting responsibly. In an era where sexual responsibility is much talked about if not practised, it is hard to know what more grotesque message about the role of women such an attitude sends out.

More disturbingly, as the tone of discourse more generally becomes cruder and more sexualised, some of the attacks on pro-life women in recent years have verged on sexual harassment. When actress and Planned Parenthood supporter Kathy Griffin[19] expressed her desire "personally" to perform pap smears on female Republican candidates, it did not seem to occur to any news outlet that what she was expressing was a form of sexual aggression.

---

[18] The event was reported by two undercover activists for the pro-life youth blog *Why I Am Pro-Life*: "Abortion Rights Offer Young People a Bleak and Nasty Vision of Life", 19 June 2012, http://whyiamprolife.blogspot .co.uk/2012/06/abortion-rights-offer-young-people.html.

[19] Carey Purcell, "Kathy Griffin Still Wants a Tony ... And She Says She's After You, Lin-Manuel Miranda and Gloria Estefan!", *Playbill*, 29 September 2015, http://www.playbill.com/article/kathy-griffin-still-wants-a-tony-and -she-says-shes-after-you-lin-manuel-miranda-and-gloria-estefan-com-364406.

If a man had expressed such a gleeful desire to perform an intimate and invasive medical test on a specific woman—even in jest—he would quite reasonably be denounced as a pervert.

However crass this sort of behaviour may be, when comedienne Laura Levites responded to a pro-life congress-woman's speech with: "I want to rip out the uterus of that pro life—Cathy McMorris Rodgers and eat it, so I can see the surprised look on her frigid face,"[20] she was arguably less offensive than those who suggest that women who oppose abortion are brainwashed, traitors or men in disguise. Levites at least acknowledged that she was dealing with another woman, albeit a woman she had the urge to cannibalise.

Women Who Regret

Any activist for a controversial cause can be expected to take abuse, and the subject of abortion is one of the most incendiary. However, of all the groups of women who oppose abortion, none pose more of a threat to abortion's compassionate image than those who stand up and say "been there, done that ... and I regret it." Rather than have the courage or honesty to listen to the grievances of women who have negative experiences of abortion, every possible effort is made to discredit them. Typically, these women are dismissed as crazy, probably suffering from some underlying mental illness, or worse, as narcissistic attention-seekers.

[20] Steven Ertelt, "Abortion Activist: 'I Want to Rip the Uterus Out of Cathy McMorris Rodgers and Eat It'", LifeNews.com, 30 January 2014, http://www.lifenews.com/2014/01/30/abortion-activist-i-want-to-rip-the-uterus-out-of-cathy-mcmorris-rogers-and-eat-it/.

Considering the wealth of evidence—some of it extremely harrowing—from women struggling after abortion, it is difficult to take seriously the accusation that women make up traumatic responses to abortion to gain an unenviable place on a pro-life platform or simply to irritate abortion campaigners. This is particularly so when one considers the hostility women face when they speak out and the dirty tactics used to silence them. British journalist Julie Burchill's response to women with postabortion trauma was sadly not unusual: "You choose to feel that way because you are weak and vain and you think your pain is important."[21] Rachael McNair states in her paper on the psychology of abortion: "It struck me that blaming the woman, making the emotional aftermath her fault, was perilously close to what batterers do to their victims. . . . Even clinic workers judge these women harshly."[22]

The problem may surround the chauvinistic notion that women should be pathetically grateful to abortion facilities for solving their problems for them. The abortion scenario has shades of Victorian melodrama about it with the pregnant woman cast as the needy victim rescued by a benevolent (and usually male) doctor who saves her from her perilous situation whilst gallantly shielding her from the gory details. When women turn on the abortion industry and state unequivocally that abortion did *not* solve their problems and certainly did not empower them to move on with their lives, there is a tendency in rebuttals of postabortive groups to treat such women as spoilt children who have been ungrateful enough to attack those who

[21] Julie Burchill, "Abortion: Still a Dirty Word", *Guardian*, 24 May 2002, http://www.theguardian.com/lifeandstyle/2002/may/25/weekend.julie burchill.

[22] McNair's work is cited in Anthony Ozimic's M.A. thesis "The Effect of Abortion on Moral Character" (St Mary's University College, 2005).

only had their best interests at heart. Rather than treating the views of a regretful woman with the respect and consideration to which she has a right, abortion promoters are quick to respond by apportioning blame and suggesting that "normal" women are happy with their abortions.

McNair is correct to suggest that the tendency to denigrate and blame women who regret their abortions is "perilously close" to the behaviour of abusers, but I would argue that it goes further than that. The hateful behaviour shown towards postabortive women is virtually *identical* to the way abusers treat their victims: the apportioning of blame, the veiled claims of attention-seeking or being a crybaby, the lies and manipulation, the attempts at painting postabortive women as suffering from any number of syndromes (except postabortion syndrome), the use of ridicule and hate-fuelled bullying. On close examination, every tactic used by abortion supporters to silence postabortive women mirrors precisely the tactics used by abusers to shame their victims into silence, down to forcing victims to question their own sanity.

No one claims that every woman who has ever had an abortion is traumatised by the experience, but those who are should surely be permitted the right to speak out without fear of bullying or judgement. The same is true of women who regret their involvement in abortion. Planned Parenthood (PP) willingly gave Abby Johnson a voice to defend abortion in the media, but as soon as she experienced a change of heart and resigned from her position as a PP clinic director, Planned Parenthood's first move was to try to use the courts to silence her.[23] Planned Parenthood was under no obligation to give a defector a platform, but

---

[23] Abby Johnson, *UnPlanned*, audiobook on CD (Carol Stream, Ill.: Tyndale, 2010).

to attempt (unsuccessfully) to prevent a woman from exercising freedom of speech was hardly acceptable from an organisation that claims to believe in women's rights.

The Colonisation of the Intellect

Former Irish president Mary McAleese claims in the book *Swimming against the Tide*:

> The myth that to be feminist is to be pro-choice has forced many women to resign from the name of feminism, to settle back bruised into the silence of the margins, victims of a new colonisation of the intellect. Why feminism should appear to be so uncomfortable with diversity and even conflict within itself on this issue is probably due more to its relative immaturity as a political and social force than anything more formidable.[24]

Whereas it is possible to argue that radical feminism has reached levels of despotism in its silencing of dissent that would be branded patriarchal and even fundamentalist coming from any other movement, it is not enough to blame this approach to dissent as mere immaturity. The forces behind the silencing of women have been too aggressive and too calculating to be explained away so easily. And the effects have been devastating both for society and—ironically—for women.

While women are driven to "the silence of the margins" by extreme hostility within feminism, the alleged fragility of women is being used to silence debate in other forums where robust exchanges of ideas should be most welcome.

[24] Angela Kennedy, ed., *Swimming against the Tide* (Dublin, Ireland: Four Courts Press, 1997), p. v.

The paternalistic casting of women as vulnerable and in need of keeping in padded comfort zones or "safe spaces" is part of a broader social problem, the steady creep of the culture of victimhood and the assertion of the spurious right to be protected from any unsettling or uncomfortable situation. The abortion debate is by no means the only one to have been silenced on university campuses, out of fear that an individual's tender feelings might be hurt, but it has been a major casualty, thanks in part to the highly sensitive nature of the subject itself. However, it is horrifying to contemplate that freedom of speech in Britain and elsewhere is coming under attack because of an assumption that women are not capable of being challenged.

As Tim Black wrote in response to the cancellation of an abortion debate at Oxford: "People, you see, particularly those to whom subordinate identities ... have been attributed, are not strong enough, not resilient enough to hear challenging arguments. They are too traumatised, too liable to 'triggering', too morally weak, too susceptible to harm.... In short, their feelings will be hurt. And so those good campaigning students are silencing debates on their behalf, on behalf of their right not to be upset, offended, or discomfited. After all, their 'comfort' is paramount."[25]

The idea behind the issuing of trigger warnings is not in itself false or a necessary enemy of freedom of speech. When trigger warnings first appeared on feminist blogs and websites, it was usually to warn about content involving sexual assault, a subject that can obviously cause a powerful trauma response to a woman who has been through assault.

[25] Tim Black, "Oxford, Abortion and the Closing of the Western Mind", *Spiked*, Free Speech Now! project, 2 February 2015, http://www.spiked -online.com/freespeechnow/fsn_article/oxford-abortion-and-the-closing-of -the-western-mind#.VyjOejArLIU.

It is unlikely anyone initially intended trigger warnings or safe space policies to include threatening to throw a female student out of a meeting for raising a hand in disagreement or shaking her head.[26] However, what began as little more than content warnings, similar to those given at the start of films or news reports, has been allowed to descend into a culture of emotional hysteria from which women have emerged very much the losers, the weak, helpless victims of society once again.

The idea that these false stereotypes of women should be bandied about at all should provoke howls of protest from feminist groups—that these stereotypes are being used to attack freedom of speech in the name of protecting women is surely beyond the pale in any twenty-first century democracy. Instead, feminist groups have allowed the "trigger warning" culture to flourish, knowing that it reinforces the most damaging gender stereotypes from which women have fought for decades to be liberated.

One has to ask the question, is this how democracy dies? Not with a bang but with a self-pitying whimper?

Out of the Margins

Human nature tends towards conformity, and even radical movements eventually come to expect conformity from members, however diverse the movement's beginnings. In her account of the use of fictitious surveys to sway public opinion on abortion, Browder quotes Bernard Nathanson's admission that the abortion movement made false

[26]Jessica Chasmar, "U.K. Student Slapped with 'Safe Space Complaint' After Raising Hand during Discussion", *Washington Times*, 4 April 2016, http://www.washingtontimes.com/news/2016/apr/4/imogen-wilson -uk-student-slapped-with-safe-space-c/.

claims that the majority favoured a change in the abortion laws prior to *Roe v. Wade* when the truth was very different: "This is the tactic of the self-fulfilling lie. Few people care to be in the minority."[27]

Whereas few choose willingly to stand for an unpopular position, all new political and ideological movements begin as a result of the courage of a minority—sometimes a minority of one. The first step is away from the "silence of the margins", and this is the crucial first step pro-life feminism has made. The first purpose of pro-life feminism is to give a platform to women denied the right to speak within the increasingly dictatorial and oppressive boundaries of mainstream feminism. These include women who regret their abortions or who have turned their backs on the abortion industry after years of doing its dirty work, but more broadly the millions of anonymous women who believe in the fundamental right to life of all members of the human family and see this belief as central to their belief in equality for women. As pro-life feminism becomes more vocal within the abortion debate, it is becoming more commonplace to hear members of the new generation of pro-life feminists questioning the authoritarian attitudes that have kept them silent in the past: "Have the oppressed become the oppressors? As victims of bullying, are women really ok with becoming bullies themselves? I'd like to think that we are better than that and that's why I am a pro-life feminist."[28]

---

[27] Browder, *Subverted*, p. 57.

[28] Sarah Delap, "First Person: I'm Pro-Life for the Same Reason I'm a Feminist", *Oxford Students for Life* (blog), 3 February 2015, http://blog .oxfordstudentsforlife.co.uk/2015/02/03/first-person-im-pro-life-for-the -same-reason-im-a-feminist/.

Abortion, Misogyny and Turning a Blind Eye

Be innocent of the knowledge, dearest chuck.

—Shakespeare, *Macbeth*

Abortionists are the self-proclaimed defenders of women's rights, an elevated position that is rarely subjected to scrutiny. There is an underlying assumption in much of the rhetoric that abortion is a wholly acceptable and necessary part of women's empowerment, meaning that proponents of abortion can only have women's best interests at heart. Abortion proponents take it upon themselves to speak for women and to act as crusaders in the name of women everywhere, without paying a great deal of attention to women who challenge this behaviour.

"Not in my name" has become a cliché used by groups of people who wish publicly to disassociate themselves from ideological positions or policies with which they are falsely assumed to agree. In recent times the banner of Not in My Name has been used by Muslims opposing ISIS,[1] men against domestic violence,[2] Jews against

[1] "#NotInMyName: ISIS Do Not Represent British Muslims", Active Change Foundation, accessed 9 February 2017, http://www.isisnotinmyname .com/.

[2] " 'Not in My Name' Campaign to Recruit Male Ambassadors to Speak Out against Domestic Abuse", Women's Institute, accessed 9 February 2017, https://www.thewi.org.uk/wi-in-wales/current-campaigns/no-more -violence-against-women/not-in-my-name-campaign-to-recruit-male -ambassadors-to-speak-out-against-domestic-abuse.

Zionism,[3] politicians against the bombing of Syria.[4] The list is endless, but there may be space left on the list of disaffected groups for pro-life feminists who are expected to sit back and watch abortion being promoted whilst their own opposition is repeatedly disregarded or silenced.

Pro-life feminists have a duty to raise that otherwise tired banner, not just because of the injustice of abortion but because of the inherent misogyny behind the assumption that women "need" abortion and are desperate to be rescued by abortion promoters from the uniquely female horror of pregnancy. So many of the arguments in favour of abortion assume that women today are growing up in a parallel universe akin to a Victorian melodrama, where pregnancy is inevitable—little different to catching a cold—and where women themselves are lost, hapless souls with no feasible alternatives to abortion and no ability to live independently.

The constant references to illegal abortion which inevitably form part and parcel of the "desperate, needy women" argument demonstrate a very basic lapse in logic by abortion promoters. The assumption is that pro-life feminists have a specific objection to *legal* abortion and therefore could not care less about women dying at the hands of backstreet butchers, when opposition to abortion by definition means opposition to abortion whatever the legal framework (this assumption tends to be made about all pro-life campaigners, who are treated as a homogeneous

[3] Ray Filar, "Why I Am an Anti-Zionist Jew", Transformation, 29 April 2016, https://www.opendemocracy.net/transformation/ray-filar/why-i-am -antizionist-jew.

[4] Jill Castle, "Not in My Name: SNP MPs Apologise to Syria for Air Strikes on Twitter after 57 of Scotland's 59 MPs Oppose Bombing", *Herald*, 3 December 2015, http://www.heraldscotland.com/news/14120866.Not_in _my_name__SNP_MPs_apologise_to_Syria_for_air_strikes_on_Twitter_after _57_of_Scotland_s_59_MPs_oppose_bombing/.

group by opponents, but my concern here is the position of pro-life feminists specifically). When abortion promoters exclaim: "I'll see you in the backalley!" the only obvious response is: "You certainly will!" However much an individual may disapprove of the pro-life position, honesty demands that the consistency of that position is taken seriously. Is it likely that a campaigner who reminds the public that abortion stops a beating heart will fight the stopping of a beating heart in a licenced clinic but will have no qualms about the stopping of a beating heart on a kitchen table? Both pro-abortion and pro-life activists are united in an abhorrence of the backstreet.

From a pro-life feminist perspective, there are three aspects of the backstreet abortion argument (a central plank of the argument for abortion more generally) which ring alarm bells in terms of the connection between abortion and unwitting misogyny. I am prepared to concede that the misogynistic reasoning behind the abortion argument is largely unintentional, but this in no way exonerates those who put forward such arguments without examining their own underlying assumptions and prejudices.

The first aspect is the deliberately exaggerated figures for illegal abortion which are discussed elsewhere. The calculated manipulation or fabrication of data is always and at all times inexcusable, denying women the right to know the true context within which abortion was legalised in many countries.

Second, as I have already hinted, suggesting that abortion provides the only plausible solution to an unintended or unwanted pregnancy is ignorant and deceptive. No one denies that illegal abortions occur and have occurred—including in countries where abortion is legal—but to suggest that there are no compassionate alternatives to abortion is not only incorrect; it distracts attention away from the thornier accompanying questions: How can it be justifiable to end a human life merely because it is unwanted? Can doctors justify to themselves intentionally ending a human life even if it is to prevent a woman endangering her own life in the act of destroying another? If a mother demanded that a doctor give her newborn baby a lethal injection and threatened to commit suicide if he would not agree to her demand, no doctor worthy of his qualification would concede, though he would hopefully do everything in his power to help the woman find a nonviolent solution to her problems.

Former abortionist Dr Beverly McMillan talks in candid terms about her exposure as a junior doctor to the reality of backstreet abortion. She writes:

> As soon as the sun went down, the elevator started coming up from the Emergency Room depositing women on our doorstep. All these women had very similar situations. They were all bleeding, running a fever, and had a tender enlarged uterus.
>
> I was puzzled, but kept working. I just basically tried to shuffle through to get them in bed and stabilized and keep up with the elevator. About halfway through that evening it finally hit me that these women were coming from the back alley abortion mills in Chicago. . . .
>
> Every night I was on call some 15 to 25 women would come in and we would take these women back, one at a time, to a little treatment room where, without any anesthesia at all, we would have to do another D & C and we would have to scrape out whatever infected tissue the abortionist had left in. It was a pretty brutal situation.
>
> I remember that at the end of the six weeks, I was very angry. It occurred to me that if women were so desperate about an unwanted pregnancy that they were willing to go to some back alley and put their life on the line, I was ready for the medical profession to start offering a

little real help to these women and show a little social responsibility.[5]

Dr McMillan's story is not unusual. She sincerely desired to help women and, following *Roe vs. Wade*, she set up shop providing abortions. However, she eventually had to confront the tiny bodies she was removing from women's wombs every day of her working life and resigned from her facility. Dr McMillan's sense of outrage at the abuse of women at the hands of backstreet abortionists did not blind her to the violence she was committing to unborn babies, nor did her rejection of abortion cause her to forget the suffering of women who experienced a botched abortion. For those who have the courage to acknowledge the reality of what they are doing, there is no getting around the fact that abortion ends a human life that is by definition innocent, and this is a moral line that cannot be crossed by a member of the medical profession—however compelling the incentive. To fail to acknowledge this is to fall once again into the trap of ignoring the macabre reality of what abortion involves and what doctors actually do when they perform abortions.

The third and most troubling aspect of the necessity argument is the widely accepted assumption that abortions will always occur and should therefore not be the subject of legal restrictions. On the face of it, this is an eminently plausible position which turns the abortion argument away from the moral issues surrounding abortion and towards a supposedly pragmatic approach to an inevitable problem. This logic could be applied to any attack on women from rape to domestic abuse. The majority of rapists and wife-beaters are never convicted or even called to account

[5] Beverly McMillan, "Former Abortionist: Dr Beverly McMillan", Lifezone, ProLife Ireland, 2018, http://www.prolifeinfo.ie/abortion-facts/providers/former-abortionists/dr-beverly-mcmillan/.

in a court of law. But would anyone honestly argue, on grounds of pragmatism, that rape and domestic violence should be decriminalised on the grounds that a certain proportion of the male population will always feel compelled to rape or batter women and it is therefore unrealistic to try to criminalise such activity? According to Britain's National Society for the Protection of Cruelty to Children (NSPCC), one in twenty children in the UK suffer sexual abuse[6] and one in fourteen experience physical abuse.[7] Arguing in terms of sheer numbers, would any adult who cares about the safety of children make a case for giving up on child protection laws as a lost cause and legislate instead for practical, pragmatic laws offering safe spaces to adults who feel the need to victimise children?

It is clearly very emotive to equate illegal abortion with other illegal activities such as rape and abuse, but the pragmatism argument is itself as emotive as it is dangerous. Any law intended to protect the vulnerable could be challenged on the grounds that it is difficult to enforce, but few would wish to see the law weakened on such grounds. The answer is surely to prevent the situations in which such outrages occur and to enforce the law as vigorously as possible.

Not in Front of the Ladies!

One of the major reasons why chivalry has been criticised and discouraged by feminists has been because it is regarded

---

[6] "Sexual Abuse: What Is Sexual Abuse", NSPCC, accessed 9 February 2017, https://www.nspcc.org.uk/preventing-abuse/child-abuse-and-neglect /child-sexual-abuse/.

[7] "Physical Abuse: Facts and Statistics", NSPCC, accessed 9 February 2017, https://www.nspcc.org.uk/preventing-abuse/child-abuse-and-neglect/physical -abuse/physical-abuse-facts-statistics/.

as a form of well-intentioned or "soft" chauvinism. Those acts of kindness (opening a door for a lady, offering a seat on the train, paying the bill, etc.) may appear respectful and considerate but, some feminists might argue, they perpetuate the idea that women are inferior to men and in need of protection or special treatment; that is, a woman cannot be expected to pay her own way, is too delicate to stand for any length of time on the train, needs to be cossetted and treated like a pet or a porcelain doll. Other women will counter and say that chivalry is a sign of good manners which puts women on a pedestal, a form of enhancing not demeaning a woman's status.

However, one expression that has virtually disappeared from modern discourse is the embarrassed warning "We're in mixed company!" or "Please, there are ladies present!" Traditionally, the warning was intended to stop another man swearing or bringing up an unsavoury topic of conversation in female company. As with other aspects of chivalry, the censoring of conversation may have been intended to avoid embarrassing or insulting the women present but could also be interpreted as placing women on a par with children. Whereas the overwhelming majority would respect the need to avoid discussing certain subjects in front of impressionable children, the notion that women are too fragile and immature to cope with adult conversation has been mercifully abandoned by all outside the "trigger warning" movement (discussed elsewhere).

A notable exception to the rule that women should be treated as robust, independent adults, equal to men, occurs whenever the subject of abortion rears its head. A common tactic to silence any discussion of abortion, even within church circles, is the warning that "it might upset women, especially women who've had abortions", as though women are too delicate to cope with such a subject and need shielding from its ugly reality by alpha males.

The misogynist belief that women need protecting from the truth about abortion is evident in details such as the literature produced by abortion facilities in which the authors euphemistically refer to the "gentle suction"[8] required to relieve a woman of the "productions of conception". It is instructive to compare the patronising, almost coaxing tone employed to describe the abortion procedure, with descriptions written for patients of elective caesarean, hernia repair or even tooth extraction.

Like nervy children, women considering abortion are reassured that "a gentle suction method is used to remove the pregnancy from the uterus",[9] "a suction machine will be used to gently complete the evacuation",[10] the Dilapan works by "gently opening the cervix"[11] and the cervix must be prepared "to cause it to gently dilate over a few hours".[12] I have never seen the word "gentle" used so frequently and so pointedly in medical literature except in the apparently factual, no-nonsense materials put out by abortion facilities. It is difficult to see how women can be expected to feel empowered if they are treated like panicky infants in need of constant reassurance that it will all

[8] "What Is Abortion?", British Pregnancy Advisory Service, 2015, https://www.bpas.org/abortion-care/considering-abortion/what-is-abortion/.

[9] "What Is a Surgical Abortion?", Marie Stopes UK, accessed 10 February 2017, https://www.mariestopes.org.uk/women/abortion/surgical-abortion-explained/what-surgical-abortion.

[10] "Dilation and Evacuation: Plan to Be at the Clinic for the Whole Day", British Pregnancy Advisory Service, 2015, https://www.bpas.org/abortion-care/abortion-treatments/surgical-abortion/dilatation-and-evacuation/.

[11] "Preparing the Cervix", British Pregnancy Advisory Service, 2015, https://www.bpas.org/abortion-care/abortion-treatments/surgical-abortion/preparing-the-cervix/.

[12] "What Is a Surgical Abortion?", Marie Stopes UK, accessed 10 February 2017, https://www.mariestopes.org.uk/women/abortion/surgical-abortion-explained/what-surgical-abortion.

be very gentle, rather than grown women capable of hearing the facts.

Abby Johnson, the former Planned Parenthood clinic director, describes in excruciating detail what happened to her when she went through a medical abortion whilst working as a student volunteer for Planned Parenthood.[13] The chasm between what she was told would happen and what happened when she took the pills was so huge, Abby assumed she had had an abnormal reaction to the drugs. She had been reassured that it would be "nothing worse than a heavy period", but what she experienced was so macabre that she refused to suggest medical abortion to women at her facility for years afterwards. She experienced severe and prolonged pain, heavy bleeding including massive blood clots, vomiting and profuse sweating. At one point, she describes her bathroom as resembling a crime scene, which she notes was a little ironic. What clearly shocked her the most was the response she received from the clinic when she described her ordeal. She was told that it was not unusual but "we don't want to scare them." If abortion promoters regard women as too infantile to be given the uncensored truth, it is difficult to see on what basis they can speak of giving women an informed choice—and a choice that is not informed is no choice at all. There is an element of "don't worry your pretty little heads with this, my dears" or Macbeth's ominous warning to his wife "be innocent of the knowledge, dearest chuck." Women are not emotionally stunted by nature, nor are they neo-Victorian ladies too delicate to participate in an adult conversation, but every time the unsavoury details

---

[13] "Abby Johnson: Planned Parenthood Kept Me in the Dark on My Abortion", LifeNews.com, 20 October 2011, http://www.lifenews.com/2011/10/20/abby-johnson-planned-parenthood-kept-me-in-the-dark-on-my-abortion/.

of abortion are deliberately hidden from women, abortion promoters perpetuate the stereotype of women as fragile and in need of protection.

Turning a Blind Eye

Whilst women are denied informed choice, the ideology of choice is being used not only to silence dissent within the feminist movement, but to paralyse any significant resistance to injustices facing women that involve abortion. In the United States, evidence has emerged in recent years revealing the level at which atrocities involving abortion have a tendency to be completely ignored or covered up even when they involve (as they invariably do) women getting hurt or killed.

Carol Everett, a former abortion facility owner, talks candidly about how systematically they lied to women and how indifferent they were to the health and safety of the women who came to them. They did not have to be careful, she admitted in an interview, if a woman became so seriously ill that she required emergency treatment; the doctors at the local hospital were happy to cover-up the records and ask no questions about how the woman had got into such a state in the first place.[14]

In 2012, abortionist Steven Brigham, a doctor with a long history of providing substandard care, was charged along with an associate with a number of serious offences. One case to emerge from the investigation was of a teenage girl, identified only as D.B., who was accompanied for a late abortion by her mother, during which her uterus

---

[14] Interview as part of the documentary *Blood Money: The Business of Abortion*, TAH, 14 May 2010.

was perforated and the remains of the dead baby shoved into her abdominal cavity, whilst part of her bowel was pulled out. Staff refused to call an ambulance, and D.B. was eventually taken to hospital in a car. The two abortionists refused to identify themselves or cooperate, leaving their maimed patient after just ten minutes. She was in such a serious condition that she had to be transported by helicopter to another hospital, where she received emergency surgery.[15] Both Brigham and his associate, Nicola Riley, avoided trial, even though many of the details surrounding the investigation into Brigham's facilities bore chilling similarities to Gosnell's House of Horrors. When accounting for his actions before a medical disciplinary hearing, Brigham continued to posture as a champion of women, insisting he should be seen as one who had "taken up the cause of women's rights and women's freedom".[16]

This appalling treatment of a woman by an abortion facility should have met with vocal, outraged condemnation from women's groups, but it was met instead with the silence of collusion. The few commentators who discussed the case at all glossed over the gory details (it is not normally in the nature of feminist dialogue to be quite so coy) and were quick to point the finger of blame at antiabortion protesters and the stigma associated with abortion. It is difficult to work out the bizarre Alice in Wonderland logic at work

[15] Cassie Farrell, "Feminism: You're Doing It Wrong ...", *LifeSite* (blog), 6 January 2012, http://www.lifesitenews.com/blog/feminism-youre-doing-it-wrong. More detailed accounts of Brigham's arrest and later appearance before a medical board can be found at "Dr. Steven Brigham Arrested Charged with Murder in Late-Term Abortions Case", WJLA Local News, 30 December 2011, http://wjla.com/news/local/dr-steven-brigham-arrested-charged-witih-murder-70864.

[16] Susan Livio, "N.J. Medical Board Revokes Abortion Doctor's License", NJ.com, 8 October 2014, http://www.nj.com/politics/index.ssf/2014/10/nj_board_revokes_abortion_doctors_license.html.

when such cases emerge, in which the heartless and wholly incompetent behaviour of abortion providers becomes the fault of the very people who speak out against it.

Dr Kermit Gosnell, his wife and a number of colleagues have been called to account and received lengthy jail sentences for running what has been dubbed a "house of horrors".[17] For years, Gosnell ran a filthy and dangerous abortion facility in which unqualified staff were employed, lifesaving equipment was permanently broken, fire exits blocked, blood and baby parts strewn about, animals wandered in and out defecating on the floor, illegal late-term abortions were routinely carried out and babies who survived the abortion procedure were murdered by having their spinal cords severed by a doctor who joked about the way their tiny bodies twitched as they died. Women were maimed and killed, with witnesses claiming that white women were given notably better treatment than the black or Asian women who came to Gosnell's clinic. Anne Furedi of BPAS (British Pregnancy Advisory Service) has been prepared to admit publicly that women going to Gosnell's facility appear to have received "shoddy

---

[17] In spite of the media blackout, the Gosnell case was reported by a number of news outlets in the United States and abroad. Here are just a few examples: Conor Friedersdorf, "Why Dr. Kermit Gosnell's Trial Should Be a Front-Page Story", *Atlantic*, 12 April 2013, http://www.theatlantic.com/national /archive/2013/04/why-dr-kermit-gosnells-trial-should-be-a-front-page -story/274944/; Terence P. Jeffrey, "Abortionist Slit Necks of Born Babies in Front of a Teenager; Told Assistant: 'That's What You Call a Chicken with Its Head Cut Off'", CNSNews.com, 13 April 2013, http://cnsnews.com/news /article/abortionist-slit-necks-born-babies-front-teenager-told-assistant-thats -what-you-call; Lydia Warren and David McCormack, "'We Plunged the Sink and a Baby's Arm Came Out': Cop Reveals Shocking Discovery Inside Abortionist's 'House of Horrors'—and How Killer Doctor Played Chopin as Police Searched His Home", *Daily Mail*, 16 May 2013, http://www.dailymail .co.uk/news/article-2325714/Dr-Kermit-Gosnell-case-We-plunged-sink -babys-arm-came-reveals-cop.html.

service",[18] which is perhaps the closest an abortion advocate can bring herself to confronting the full horror of Gosnell's actions.

One former patient of Gosnell has spoken publicly about her distress at being informed by the authorities that one of many pairs of baby feet Gosnell kept in jars as trophies belonged to her aborted baby, and that she would never have gone through with it if she had been told the truth—that she was in fact much further along with the pregnancy than she had realised.

That particular deception was verified by Steven Massof,[19] an unlicenced physician who was sentenced to between six and twelve years' imprisonment for the murder of two newborn babies. In evidence against his former employer, Massof admitted that ultrasound images were manipulated to convince the woman that the pregnancy was less advanced than it really was. He also stated that he witnessed the killing of over one hundred babies who survived the abortion procedure and described the killings as "literally a beheading".

The Gosnell case is far and away the most serious to have emerged in recent years, though it is certainly not an isolated case in terms of abortionists maiming and abusing women. What is in many ways most shocking about this devastating case is the lengthy cover-up, not just by departments and organisations which had the power (not to mention the duty) to expose Gosnell, but by the media itself.

[18] "USA: Doctor Charged with Illegal Abortions", *Abortion Review*, 25 January 2011, http://www.abortionreview.org/index.php/site/article/910/.

[19] "Assistant at Philadelphia Abortion 'House of Horrors' Clinic Gets 6–12 Years for Role in Which He Saw Aborted Babies Routinely Killed with Scissors", *Daily Mail*, http://www.dailymail.co.uk/news/article-2558092/Assistant -Philadelphia-abortion-house-horrors-gets-6-12-years.html?printingPage=true.

Journalists have admitted that the conspicuous media silence in reporting what may well be the worst case of medical mass murder in American history is completely deliberate. A segment on HuffPost Live included the admission: "For what it's worth, I do think that those of us on the left have made a decision not to cover this trial because we worry that it'll compromise abortion rights. Whether you agree with abortion or not, I do think there's a direct connection between the media's failure to cover this and our own political commitments on the left. I think it's a bad idea, I think it's dangerous, but I think that's the way it is."[20]

That's the way it is? An abortionist who exploited, abused and risked the lives of women for seventeen years, who snapped the necks of hundreds of newborn babies, has been protected by the media in the name of "rights"? I cannot be the only woman to feel that "that's the way it is" just is not good enough.

Following his initial conviction, Gosnell has also been sentenced to thirty years for running a "pill mill" in which he illegally dispensed hundreds of thousands of painkillers which were then sold on the street by dealers and addicts.[21] Despite being convicted of so many crimes, Dr Kermit Gosnell has expressed no remorse whatsoever for his actions or concern for the harm he has caused. According to an interview from prison, he sees himself as "spiritually innocent", a brave doctor persecuted by the establishment

---

[20] Erik Wemple, "Gosnell Case: HuffPost Host Says Left 'Made a Decision' to Not Cover Trial", *Washington Post*, 16 April 2013, https://www .washingtonpost.com/blogs/erik-wemple/wp/2013/04/16/gosnell-case -huffpost-host-says-left-made-a-decision-to-not-cover-trial/.

[21] Allie Malloy, "Philadelphia Abortion Doctor Kermit Gosnell Gets 30 Years for Pill Mill", CNN.com, 17 December 2013, http://edition.cnn.com /2013/12/16/justice/pennsylvania-abortion-doctor-pills/.

in his fight against poverty. He has even taken to writing poetry from his prison cell on the subject.[22]

For the sake of clarity, it is important to stress that Britain is far from exempt when it comes to abortion malpractice, with an MP (Member of Parliament) warning during a parliamentary debate on the Abortion Act: "I put it to the Attorney-General that given the infinitesimally low rate of prosecutions for illegal abortions ... we live in a situation where doctors, frankly, can get away with it."[23] He was referring to both the decision not to prosecute doctors who were filmed agreeing to sex-selective abortion and an investigation which found that at fourteen separate locations, the Abortion Act was being routinely flouted.

A number of attempts have been made in Britain to challenge the many instances in which the law has been broken by doctors, few of which have ever resulted in a conviction, and those that have never go beyond a slap on the wrist—for example, in 2001, Anglican pastor Joanna Jepson failed in her attempt to prosecute doctors who had performed an abortion on grounds that the baby had cleft palate, a condition from which she herself suffered. She argued that cleft palate did not fall within the definition of "serious handicap". In 2013, the Director of Public Prosecutions ruled against putting two doctors on trial who

[22] Brian Howard, "Exclusive: Kermit Gosnell Says He Is 'Spiritually Innocent'—and Sends Abortion-Inspired Poetry from Prison", *Philadelphia*, 23 September 2013, http://blogs.phillymag.com/the_philly_post/2013/09/23/convicted-abortion-doctor-kermit-gosnell-spiritually-innocent-ebook/. A detailed analysis of the Gosnell Case can be found in Ann McElhinney and Phelim McAleer, *Gosnell: The Untold Story of America's Most Prolific Serial Killer* (Washington, D.C., Regnery Publishing, 2017).

[23] Sir Edward Leigh, intervening during a debate on abortion (Westminster Hall, 9 October 2013), http://www.publications.parliament.uk/pa/cm201314/cmhansrd/cm131009/halltext/131009h0001.htm.

had been secretly filmed by journalists agreeing to perform sex-selective abortions.[24]

When I first started looking into this area of the abortion issue, it was impossible to avoid the consideration that some of the abuses might be an inevitable part of a culture of complacency surrounding abortion. After all, it is decades since abortion was decriminalised in countries such as Britain and the United States, and the subject may no longer be regarded as meriting a great deal of scrutiny. However, abuses of this nature appear to have occurred under the noses of health regulators for as long as abortion has been legal. An undercover investigation in the United States just six years after *Roe v. Wade* exposed a catalogue of similar horrors, including filthy conditions, professional misconduct and even the practice of performing abortions on women who were not pregnant. A woman would be told she was pregnant, pay for an abortion and go through what she thought was a surgical abortion, but in fact there was no baby in the first place.[25]

The manipulation of women when it comes to abortion does not necessarily have to involve gory stories of maimed women, blood-stained floors and murdered babies. Pro-life campaigners need to be wary of focusing too closely on the most harrowing cases as coercion can be a great deal subtler and harder to identify than that. A former office manager of a Texas abortion facility, Judy W. (surname withheld), has admitted: "If a woman we were counselling expressed doubts about having an abortion, we would say

[24] Michael Cook, "No Prosecution for Doctors Who Agreed to Sex-Selective Abortion in UK", BioEdge, 19 October 2013, http://www.bioedge .org/bioethics/bioethics_article/10728.

[25] Pamela Zekman and Pamela Warrick, "The Abortion Profiteers", *Chicago Sun-Times*, 12–28 November, 1978, http://dlib.nyu.edu/undercover/abortion -profiteers-pamela-zekman-pamela-warrick-chicago-sun-times.

whatever was necessary to persuade her to have the abortion immediately.... The abortion clinic that I managed was strictly a business operation.... We did not consider the well-being of the women who had abortions."[26]

Clarissa, a former abortion facility employee, talks about the way her facility treated the women who came to it for abortions:

> The girls who were unsure were lied to and coerced into killing their babies. They were told it was safe, they were not informed of their options, and they were never told about how they would feel afterwards. The girls that were only a month or two along would be given pills that would kill the baby and told they would have heavy bleeding. They were never told that they were going to be flushing their babies down the toilet. The girls who were farther along, they were given two medications, one so they wouldn't feel anything, the other one so they wouldn't remember. The medications did not always work. They were held down by the abortionist's assistants, screaming in agony, as their babies were ripped apart and pulled out with a vacuum. If they were ever to change their minds, they were told that it was too late. When the medicine did work, the abortionist and his assistants would laugh, tell jokes, and even watch TV while they were killing the babies. Afterwards, the girls were ushered out the back door in varying conditions, some barely able to walk, vomiting, confused, high on their medications, and crying hysterically.[27]

---

[26] Anthony Ozimic, "The Effect of Abortion on Moral Character" (master's thesis, St Mary's University College, Twickenham, 2005).

[27] Sarah Terzo, "Clinic Worker on Women Getting Abortions: 'They All Had Sadness in Their Eyes'", LifeNews.com, 10 January 2014, http://www.lifenews.com/2014/01/10/clinic-worker-on-women-getting-abortions-they-all-had-sadness-in-their-eyes/.

In October 2013, a young woman called Melinda posted her story on a social networking site. She had decided to go through abortion because she was pregnant with triplets and felt unable to care for three babies, but changed her mind about having the abortion after witnessing a March for Life where she realised that there was a lot of help and support available. It is a point of interest in itself that she was given information about possible alternatives by "anti-choice fanatics" and not from the abortion facility itself. Melinda writes:

> When I walked into the clinic on Monday morning to cancel my appointment with them, I was told to sit down and wait for the doctor to come and see me.
> I refused and said I was leaving, and was told I had already signed everything and couldn't back out now. The counsellor came out and I felt relief, I told her I had changed my mind and was keeping my babies. She did not smile back and the doctor finally emerged, they exchanged quick glances—The doctor looked annoyed and the counsellor looked ... ashamed. They started talking in low voices, kept glancing at me. I felt suddenly uneasy and headed for the door. The receptionist noticed and tried to call me back, so I ran. I ran for my life and the lives inside of me. I've never been so scared in my life.[28]

Abortion providers are keen to shed crocodile tears and claim that, like pro-lifers, they wish that there were no abortions; however, they say, the harsh reality is that abortion is a necessity they have to provide. But the disingenuous

---

[28] March for the Babies, Facebook.com, 15 October 2013, https://www.facebook.com/permalink.php?story_fbid=598009736930527&id=105936922804480.

nature of this position is not difficult to challenge. When thousands of Eastern European migrants settled in Britain following the expansion of the European Union, there was a rise in abortions among Eastern European women. One abortion facility manager admitted: "Some women have said to me that they would want to continue with the pregnancy, but they haven't been in this country for very long, and they are not entitled to the benefits. If they were entitled to that then they would continue with the pregnancy. It's sad that that is a big factor."[29]

If abortion promoters felt so sad about women being driven to abortions for financial reasons, they would surely do the decent thing and refer them to organisations which offer financial help and accommodation to pregnant women in need. The fact that they do not offer them that choice and label groups which can offer real alternatives to women as "antichoice" undermines both the sad and the necessary aspects of the argument. It is arguable that if women were given all the help and advice necessary to continue with their pregnancies, if they were told frankly what abortion involves, if abortion facilities rejoiced when a woman changed her mind rather than trying to talk her round, the abortion rate would take a nosedive with or without changes to the law.

The Closing Down of Scientific Debate

As I am neither a scientist nor an oncologist, it is not my place to put the case for an abortion–breast cancer link. In my opinion, whether or not there is a causal link between

---

[29] Angus Stickler, "Immigrant Pregnancies Stretch NHS", BBC News, 26 March 2007, http://news.bbc.co.uk/1/hi/health/6494651.stm.

induced abortion and breast cancer has little to do with the ethics of abortion itself or the case for banning abortion. The link between smoking and lung cancer is no longer controversial, but though I am broadly in favour of restrictions on smoking where it may harm others (e.g., smoking in public places), I would not ban the sale and use of tobacco because of the cancer risk.

Where the hotly contested abortion–breast cancer (ABC) link is highly relevant to the debate is when it comes to the right of women to be treated as rational adults and given full information in order to give informed consent. The impression given by the scientific community is that the ABC debate is closed, a resounding verdict of safety has been issued and the subject should not be raised again. When pro-choice filmmaker Punam Kumar Gill investigated the controversy surrounding the ABC link, she was disturbed by the extent to which politics appears to filter what women hear about abortion. She stated: "It's true, the long-term health risks associated with abortion are generally promoted by those who want abortion gone. Equally disturbing are those who deny that any long-term risks exist, which is currently the stance of all the major medical organizations."[30] The filmmakers encountered significant resistance and noncooperation from the medical establishment during the making of *Hush*, a film which explores the suppression of evidence for political reasons through interviews with doctors, scientists and postabortive women themselves.[31]

[30] "HUSH Documentary Comes to Canada", LifeCanada (2016), accessed 8 January 2018, https://lifecollective.io/lifecanada/get-involved/programs /hush-documentary-comes-to-canada.

[31] "Barbara Kay: Tough Questions on the Health Risks of Abortion Remain", *National Post*, 23 October 2015, http://news.nationalpost.com/full -comment/barbara-kay-tough-questions-on-abortion.

Individual doctors and researchers who put forward arguments and evidence to support the ABC link face a level of hostility and personal attack that has no place in modern scientific discourse. It is difficult to imagine experts such as Angela Lanfranchi and Joel Brind being treated in such a hysterical manner if they stood against the closed ranks of the establishment on any other issue. Angela Lanfranchi is dismissed as "an antiabortion advocate who continues to push the discredited idea of a link between abortion and breast cancer",[32] rather than a highly skilled and experienced doctor who has dedicated her life to treating and researching breast cancer.

The determination by feminist groups to suppress or discredit any study which appears to support the ABC link has been the subject of comment for decades. During the 1990s, columnist Joe Gelman wrote in the *L.A. Daily News*:

> So, how has the feminist establishment reacted to these findings? Stone silence or denial by some and an active campaign to discredit the findings by others. One would think that individuals and organizations committed to women's issues, particularly health issues, would be more than eager to educate the public, and specifically its own supposed constituency about the discovery of another cause of one of the most devastating diseases to afflict women in the United States and the world over.... Indeed, since the findings were published in the British Medical Association's Journal, (hardly a bastion of right-wing, pro-life propaganda), a number of smaller studies were quickly commissioned in the United States, resorting

---

[32] Melissa Davey, "Angela Lanfranchi, Who Links Abortion and Cancer, Stars at Families Congress", *Guardian*, 30 August 2014, http://www.the guardian.com/world/2014/aug/30/angela-lafranchi-who-links-abortion-and -cancer-stars-at-families-congress.

to less scientific methods, and the feminist PR machine
was set in motion in order to discredit the comprehensive
study published in the British Journal.[33]

Why the hysterical determination to ignore both the
debate and the evidence? There is an uneasy parallel here
between the strident campaign to suppress any discussion of
a potential ABC link and the lengths to which the tobacco
industry attempted to silence any discussion on a possible link between smoking and cancer. It is worth remembering that when Victorian British physician Dr Thomas
Allinson put forward the idea that smoking was dangerous
at a time when it was widely believed to be beneficial to
health (or at least not harmful), the medical community
were quick to close ranks against him and have him struck
off.[34] Feminist groups may not be obliged to take sides in
the ABC debate, but no group claiming to care for women
has any business closing down the debate itself.

Shooting the Messenger

Those who do attempt to sound the alarm about the ugly
reality of abortion can find themselves silenced in a variety
of ways, including through the might of the legal system
if necessary, in order to protect women from the right
to make an informed choice. Abby Johnson, the former Planned Parenthood clinic director turned pro-life

[33] Joe Gelman, "Findings Linking Cancer to Abortions a Well-Kept Secret",
Los Angeles Daily News, Viewpoint, 28 September 1997.
[34] "Exercise More, Don't Drink, Don't Smoke.... In 1893 Dr Allinson
Tried to Make Britian Healthier—and Was Struck Off", *Scotsman*, updated
3 January 2008, http://www.scotsman.com/news/uk/exercise-more-don't
-drink-don't-smoke-in-1893-dr-allinson-tried-to-make-britain-healthier-and
-was-struck-off-1-1072155.

campaigner, faced aggressive legal challenges to her right to speak openly about Planned Parenthood's practices. Abby Johnson's former employers worked hard using the courts to stop a professional woman saying anything that might show Planned Parenthood in a poor light, which could only give the impression that the organisation might have something to hide.

Planned Parenthood's failed attempt to gag an errant female employee pales into insignificance compared with the wholesale attempt by the same organisation to destroy an investigative journalist whose undercover footage caused outrage across the world. David Daleiden released numerous undercover videos showing Planned Parenthood employees and associates haggling over the sale of aborted baby parts. The response from Planned Parenthood and allies within the media has been a prolonged smear campaign against Daleiden intended to portray him nationally as a liar and a fraud who embarked upon a plot to lead innocent Planned Parenthood staff up the garden path. The videos themselves have been repeatedly dismissed as edited, doctored or simply an elaborate hoax. Planned Parenthood's embattled CEO Cecile Richards has gone to considerable lengths to portray her organisation as the victim of a right-wing conspiracy: "It is clear they acted fraudulently and unethically—and perhaps illegally. Yet it is Planned Parenthood, not Mr. Daleiden, that is currently subject to four separate congressional investigations."[35]

In a Kafkaesque turn of events, the same court that acquitted Planned Parenthood of selling baby parts charged Daleiden with attempting to buy them, a charge

---

[35] "Statement of Cecile Richards, President, Planned Parenthood Federation of America, before the House Committee on Oversight and Government Reform", 29 September 2015, https://oversight.house.gov/wp-content/uploads/2015/09/Richards-PPFA-Statement-9-29-Planned-Parenthood.pdf.

that surely only holds water if there were a seller involved. Common sense prevailed eventually in Daleiden's case, but it was troubling to consider that an organisation which has the backing of the liberal establishment should be prepared to silence those who reveal the ugly side of abortion by attempting to get a man imprisoned for twenty years for filming real events. I make no comment about the ethics of filming individuals without their consent or knowledge, but it is hard to imagine Daleiden receiving such harsh treatment if he had exposed unethical practices at a chain of abattoirs or in a care home. Covert filming is used on a regular basis by undercover journalists, including those employed by both campaigning organisations and respected broadcasters such as the BBC. It is worth citing, by way of comparison, the seriousness with which undercover footage of abuse in homes for the elderly was taken by Britain's Care Quality Commission,[36] and the media's willingness to accept the authenticity of videos purporting to show abuses at halal abattoirs.[37]

A Tale of Two Betrayed Women
Savita/Aisha—Every Death Diminishes
Me, but Some More Than Others

Savita's name is known around the world. A beautiful young woman pregnant with her first child, Savita

[36] "CQC Comment on Panorama—Behind Closed Doors: Elderly Care Exposed", Care Quality Commission, last updated 10 November 2014, http://www.cqc.org.uk/public/news/cqc-comment-panorama-behind -closed-doors-elderly-care-exposed.

[37] Nigel Morris, "Halal Slaughter: Outcry after Undercover Film Exposes Brutality of Industry", *Independent*, 3 February 2015, http://www.independent .co.uk/news/uk/home-news/outcry-after-undercover-film-exposes-brutality -of-halal-industry-10019467.html.

Halappanavar became seriously ill during her pregnancy and died as a result of a tragic breakdown in communication within her hospital. An investigation into her death[38] found that there were thirteen missed opportunities to save her, resulting in her needless death from complications from a septic miscarriage. There is no excuse for such a string of errors in a well-run, twenty-first-century hospital, and her death rightly provoked outrage. However, campaigners will never forget the manner in which her death was twisted into a cynical and sustained attack on Ireland's pro-life laws. Savita's tragic death became a cause celebre: in death, unable to consent to such treatment, she became a poster girl for abortion; her face appeared on banners agitating for abortion; her name was spelt out in candles at vigils. In the minds of thousands around the world, Savita became a martyr of pro-life Ireland, a young life snuffed out because Ireland would not grant her a life-saving abortion.

The result of the inquest which highlighted the real reason for Savita's needless death—administrative failures within the hospital—did nothing to separate Savita from the abortion juggernaut, and her name continues to be invoked to justify the legalisation of abortion to save the life of the mother.

Shortly after Savita's death, another young woman died tragically and needlessly. Her name was Aisha Chithira,[39]

---

[38] *Investigation into the Safety, Quality and Standards of Services Provided by the Health Service Executive to Patients, including Pregnant Women, at Risk of Clinical Deterioration, including Those Provided in University Hospital Galway, and as Reflected in the Care and Treatment Provided to Savita Halappanavar* (Dublin: Health Information and Quality Authority, 7 October 2013).

[39] "Three Medics Deny Manslaughter of Woman Who Travelled to UK for Abortion", Press Association, *Guardian*, 27 November 2015, http://www.theguardian.com/uk-news/2015/nov/27/medics-deny-manslaughter-woman-abortion-ireland-aisha-chithira.

but it is unlikely that any reader of this book will be familiar with her. Her name is virtually unknown, as are the tragic circumstances surrounding her death. Aisha travelled from Ireland to England and died of massive internal bleeding following a "safe, legal abortion" at a Marie Stopes clinic in London. There were no candlelit vigils for Aisha, her face did not adorn banners waved by outraged feminists, there were few—if any—column inches devoted to angry denunciations of those responsible for her death. Where her death was reported in the mainstream media, reports were sketchy and brief, covering the basic details of the manslaughter trial that followed and the subsequent acquittal of the doctor.

Aisha's problem was perhaps that her death did not support the right narrative—legal abortion is supposed to be a saviour of women not a killer. If she had died trying to self-abort or on the kitchen table of a backstreet abortionist, if she had died from a rare pregnancy complication, Aisha would have been worthy of the media's attention. Savita's death tugged on the heart of every woman who has ever been pregnant; she spoke for all women everywhere. Aisha's death apparently did not have the same emotional charge and did not deserve the same outpouring of sympathy. Every woman's death diminishes the sisterhood, but only when that death is politically useful.

The Greatest Bioethical Atrocity on the Globe

In today's China, under the Communist rule, the government can put their hand into your body, grab your baby out of your womb, and kill your baby in your face.

— Chen Guangcheng

This chapter is not intended as an exposé of the many atrocities committed in the name of China's birth-control policies, popularly, though inaccurately, known as the one-child policy. Many other investigators and witnesses, both perpetrators and victims of the policy, have worked courageously to draw the world's attention to the humanitarian disaster caused by China's forced population control. Steve Mosher's landmark book *A Mother's Ordeal* provides a harrowing eyewitness account of the early years of the Chinese population-control experiment from a woman (Chi An) who worked as an enforcer before falling victim to the family planning laws she had brutally imposed upon other women.

Better known is the extraordinary story of Chen Guangcheng, the blind lawyer who exposed thousands of

Reggie Littlejohn, "Chen Guangcheng's Remarks on China's One Child Policy—The Heritage Foundation", *Women's Rights without Frontiers* (blog), 4 November 2014, http://www.womensrightswithoutfrontiers.org/blog/?p =1854; comments made during a presentation given on behalf of the Heritage Foundation on 9 October 2014.

cases of forced abortion and temporarily put the spotlight on China's abuse of women. However, it is interesting to note that a man who suffered arrest, imprisonment, beatings and torture in his determination to help women has received little support from feminist organisations. Chen Guangcheng has rightly been given a number of awards for his human rights work but, as US senator Chris Smith has observed, feminist groups appear more interested in attacking a fictitious war on American women than in attacking the horrific suppression of women's rights being perpetuated in the name of population control.

Across the political spectrum, China's coercive birth-control policy has been termed "a barbaric experiment in social engineering"[1] and "the greatest bioethical atrocity on the globe".[2] Through the implementation of this policy, the Chinese authorities—with the cooperation and support of Western aid agencies—have interfered with the most intimate aspect of women's lives and deprived women of their right to family life.[3] Since 1979, women have been forced or coerced into undergoing sterilisation and abortion, threatened along with their families with financial ruin, loss of employment, imprisonment, torture

[1] Ma Jian, "China's Barbaric One-Child Policy", *Guardian*, 6 May 2013, http://www.guardian.co.uk/books/2013/may/06/chinas-barbaric-one-child -policy?fb=native&commentpage=2.

[2] Wendy McElroy, "U.S. Should Stay Out of UNESCO", Feminists.com, 24 September 2002, http://www.ifeminists.com/introduction/editorials/2002 /0924.html.

[3] The accusations made against aid agencies are too numerous to mention. Lord Alton has challenged Britain's Department for International Development (DFID) to account for how "over three decades, British aid given to UNFPA and IPPF has gone to the China Population Association. The CPA, in turn, has implemented a one-child policy that makes it a criminal offence to be pregnant and illegal to have a brother or a sister" (*House of Lords Official Report: Parliamentary Debates [Hansard]*, vol. 737, no. 6, 17 May 2012, http://www.parliament .uk/documents/TSO-PDF/lords-hansard/LHAN6.pdf).

and the destruction of their homes if they commit the crime of bringing "unauthorised" children into the world.

A common tactic used to distract attention away from China's appalling human rights record has been to suggest that abuses associated with population control *have* occurred but only in the past, when tragic reports of human rights abuses continue to emerge. The British peer Baroness Tonge used this tactic during a House of Lords debate when she spoke of "the type of coercion mentioned by the noble Lord, Lord Alton, that occurred some years ago in China"[4] whilst trying to argue the case for a "voluntary" reduction in world population. The debate in question took place in 2012 at precisely the time Chen Guangcheng's plight was receiving media attention, but Baroness Tonge appeared unaware that Chen urged a *continued* fight against injustice, not simply the acknowledgement of past wrongs.

It is difficult to believe that those who argue that human rights abuses occurred only in the past can possibly be so ignorant of the facts. Only a year before Baroness Tonge made that dismissive remark, a congressional hearing in the United States heard evidence of abuses including "forced abortion, forced sterilization, forced contraception, the demolition of homes, the use of 'implication' (detention, torture and fining of relatives of 'violators'), a couple put to torture for missing an ante-natal check-up and a man who was beaten to death because his son was suspected of having a second child."[5]

---

[4] Ibid.

[5] "Congressional Hearing—China's One Child Policy, September 22, 2011, House Committee on Foreign Affairs, Subcommittee on Africa, Global Health, and Human Rights", Women's Rights without Frontiers, accessed 10 February 2017, http://www.womensrightswithoutfrontiers.org/index.php ?nav=congressional_hearing.

One recent casualty of these punitive measures was Wang Guangrong, a thirty-seven-year-old farmer who was unable to pay the heavy fines demanded by family planning officials to register his illegal children. Without birth registration or *hukou*, a child does not exist in the eyes of the state and cannot access healthcare, education, public transport, employment or legal redress if they are the victims of criminal activity. *Hei Hazei* or black children, as hukouless children are sometimes known (black signifying being unlucky rather than a reference to ethnicity), are also vulnerable to crime, particularly abduction, as their existence is not registered. Wang Guangrong had already had his livestock confiscated by family planning officials as punishment for having unauthorised children, and his family were destitute. This was not enough for the officials, who continued to harass him and to demand another round of heavy fines as a condition of obtaining school places for his children. He broke under the strain and committed suicide in protest.[6]

Another victim of China's birth-control policies was Gong Qifeng, who at seven months' pregnant with her second child was forcibly restrained and had abortion-inducing drugs injected into her stomach as she pleaded to be left alone. After thirty-five hours in agony, she gave birth to a dead baby boy. Following her ordeal, Gong described feeling like "a walking corpse", her mental health suffered, and two years later she was diagnosed with schizophrenia.[7]

[6] Rebecca Johnson, "Father Kills Himself after Being Fined for Flouting China's One-Child Policy", *Express*, 21 May 2014, http://www.express.co .uk/news/world/477269/Tragic-truth-of-China-s-one-child-policy-dad-s -sacrifice-to-give-children-an-education.

[7] Associated Press, "Forced Abortions in China Show Abuse of Policy", 9 January 2014, http://www.news.com.au/world/forced-abortions-in-china -show-abuse-of-policy/news-story/9105c6b437017abb8036ec4c69234f42.

It is impossible to quantify the harm that has been done to thousands of women like Gong Qifeng as a result of such violent invasions of their bodily integrity. I would argue that forced abortion combines the two greatest female horrors—the violent loss of a child and rape, as forced abortion can surely be classified as a form of surgical rape. When we consider the sheer numbers of women who have been forced or coerced into abortion in China over a period of over thirty-five years, the mental health of women should be regarded as a national emergency. It cannot be considered entirely coincidental that China is the only country in the world where more women than men commit suicide every year, accounting for over half of all female suicides in the world. Suicide is currently the number-one cause of death for young women in China, with a woman committing suicide on average every four minutes.[8]

There are many factors behind China's appalling suicide statistics—poverty, isolation, the enduring stigma associated with mental illness, the poor status of women, the lack of preventative strategies—and none of these many factors should be overlooked in a discussion about suicide in China. However, it is difficult to imagine a more overwhelming attack on a woman's mental, physical and emotional well-being than coercive abortion.

The social implications of coercive birth-control policies are damaging both on an individual and on a population level. The most dangerous effect of China's population-control policy on a social and demographic level is the widespread practice of gendercide, which is discussed in another chapter, with China's rapidly ageing population

---

[8] Rebekah Nydam, "Women and Suicide in China", HubPages, updated 10 January 2015, http://hubpages.com/education/The-Problem-of-Female-Suicide-in-China.

coming a close second. However, the effects of turning the entirely natural event of giving birth into a punishable act of political defiance may brutalise a population by stealth. When abortion becomes compulsory and couples are repeatedly given the message that a baby must be sacrificed for the perceived good of the state, human lives are reduced to biological units to be snuffed out at will.

In 2013, a story hit the headlines in China about a newborn baby[9] who was rescued after being flushed down a toilet and trapped for hours in a sewage pipe. Tragically, stories of infant abandonment are not uncommon, and Baby 59, as the newborn was temporarily named, is not the only child in China to have been rescued from such a horrific fate. A similar case was reported the following year.[10] However, the case caused widespread anger and soul-searching in China and beyond, with one Chinese blogger warning: "The one-child policy has turned us all into brutes."[11] Professor Paul Yip of Hong Kong University was quoted in a British newspaper as saying: "In China, life is held cheap. This isn't a very stable foundation for society."[12]

Another incident which made international news did not end so hopefully for the infants and families concerned. In January 2014, a fifty-five-year-old obstetrician, Dr Zhang Shuxia, was sentenced to death for child trafficking. She told parents that their baby had died or was

[9] Tania Branigan, "China's Baby 59 Left in Sewage Pipe Evokes Mass Sympathy and Anger", *Guardian*, 29 May 2013, http://www.theguardian.com world/2013/may/28/china-baby-59-sewer-pipe.

[10] Sara C. Nelson, "Newborn Baby Girl Rescued from Sewer Pipe in China", *Huffington Post*, updated 18 September 2014, http://www.huffingtonpost.co.uk 2014/09/18/newborn-baby-girl-rescued-sewer-pipe-china_n_5842806.html.

[11] Hazel Knowles, "How Baby Flushed Down Toilet Was Lucky: Shocking Toll of China's One-Child Rule", *Daily Mirror*, 1 June 2013, http://www .mirror.co.uk/news/world-news/how-baby-flushed-down-toilet-1925083.

[12] Ibid.

dying, or was suffering from some severe disability and should be placed for adoption, then sold the babies to traffickers, with baby boys fetching nearly twice the sum of baby girls. This doctor's sentence was suspended, and I am not the only campaigner to feel a sense of relief that she was not put to death in spite of the seriousness of her crimes. She is thought to have sold scores of babies over a period of eight years, and at least one was found dead in a ditch, having been dumped by traffickers. There is no avoiding the horrific nature of her crimes, which have caused untold heartache to parents and deprived children of their right to be raised by their own parents; and in at least one case, Dr Shixua's actions have resulted in death. By no stretch of the imagination are this doctor's actions justifiable, but her actions are certainly no more heinous than those carried out by countless family planning officials with state approval and were made possible because of the moral and socio-economic framework created by the one-child policy. In a country without a welfare state, parents are more likely to give up a child with disabilities in order to try for a child who will be able to support them in their old age. The preference for boys has turned male babies into highly prized commodities.[13]

The baby saved from the sewage pipe was described by a *Guardian* columnist as "a grotesque image of abandonment",[14] but he might just as easily be described as a grotesque image of China's birth-control policies, the obvious consequence of a society in which "unauthorised" women

[13] "Chinese Obstetrician Zhang Shuxia Found Guilty of Trafficking Newborn Babies", *Weekend Australian*, 14 January 2014, http://www.theaustralian .com.au/news/world/chinese-obstetrician-zhang-shuxia-found-guilty -of-trafficking-newborn-babies/story-e6frg6so-1226801572081.

[14] Jonathan Jones, "China's Baby 59 Sewer Pipe Rescue Is a Grotesque Image of Abandonment", *Guardian*, 29 May 2013, http://www.theguardian .com/commentisfree/photography-blog/2013/may/29/china-baby-59 -rescue-ultimate-abandonment.

(in this case unmarried) are forced to conceal pregnancies or be forced into abortion facilities.

Apologists for China's state-enforced population control who do not dismiss the humanitarian situation as a historical detail tend to put forward one of two arguments in defence of the state's right to nationalise women's fertility: denial or necessity. The denial approach, oft-repeated in the international press, is that abuses against women including forced abortion and sterilisation *do* occur but are the result of overzealous officials rather than the fault of the policy itself. Chinese law theoretically prohibits coercion, and the "overzealous officials" argument is rooted in a determination by some groups and individuals to take the Chinese Communist Party at its word in terms of its own human rights record. The USA's Country Report on China (2013) states that extra-legal punishment is a not uncommon practice in China, including arbitrary house arrest and detention of family members, and that "citizens had limited forms of redress against official abuse". The report notes the existence of "a coercive birth-limitation policy that in some cases resulted in forced abortion (sometimes at advanced stages of pregnancy) or forced sterilization".[15] In the section on reproductive rights, the report goes into more detail:

> Although national law prohibits the use of physical coercion to compel persons to submit to abortion or sterilization, intense pressure to meet birth-limitation targets set by *government regulations* resulted in instances of local family-planning officials' using physical coercion to meet *government goals* [emphasis added]. Such practices included

[15] "Country Reports on Human Rights Practices for 2013", US Department of State, 2013, http://www.state.gov/j/drl/rls/hrrpt/humanrightsreport/index.htm?year=2013&dlid=220186#wrapper.

the mandatory use of birth control and the abortion of unauthorized pregnancies. In the case of families that already had two children, one parent was often pressured to undergo sterilization.... The country's birth-limitation policies retained harshly coercive elements in law and practice. The financial and administrative penalties for unauthorized births were strict.[16]

If local officials are indeed using excessive force, they do so under pressure from their superiors in government.

Fundamentally, the argument that China's population-control policy only results in atrocities when it is in some way misused is to ignore or fail to understand the central problem with the policy, and that is that the policy is *inherently coercive.* Any state which reserves the right to determine how many children a couple may have and under which circumstances they may have them, any state which takes it upon itself to interfere with the rights of couples to engage in an act of procreation, will enforce a policy of intrusion that will *by definition* be coercive. It will *by definition* involve the suppression of civil liberties.

This is by no means an unusual or controversial position. Chinese Human Rights Defenders (CHRD) warned in a 2010 report that previous attempts to "rein in abusive practices associated with the family planning policy" had failed and that "the family planning policy remains abusive of Chinese citizens' reproductive rights regardless of the number of children each couple is allowed to have, and will remain so unless the policy in its current form is abolished."[17]

---

[16] Ibid.

[17] "'I Don't Have a Choice over My Own Body': The Chinese Government Must End Its Abusive Family Planning Policy", Chinese Human Rights Defenders, 21 December 2010, http://chrdnet.com/wp-content/uploads/2010/12/%E2%80%9CI-Don%E2%80%99t-Have-a-Choice-over-My-Own-Body%E2%80%9D4.pdf.

Every time the Chinese authorities claim to have decided to "relax" or "loosen" the policy[18] to allow a second child in a greater number of circumstances, for example, well-intentioned individuals celebrate such announcements as evidence that the status of women is improving.[19] However, the motivation behind changes when they do occur[20] is driven more by economic reality than humanitarian considerations. A generation of "double-single" couples, sometimes also referred to as the 4-2-1 problem, has created an inverse pyramid of financial dependence, with one working adult forced to support two parents and possibly also four grandparents in the absence of siblings to share the financial burden.

Nor are any policy changes as significant as some media outlets like to believe.[21] On the last occasion Beijing announced that the one-child policy would be "relaxed", Human Rights Watch made a point of cautioning that, welcome though a change might be, human rights were still severely limited and abuses would continue.[22] In case any activist were in any doubt about the utilitarian

[18] Arnold Hou, "Heilongjiang Passes Amendment to One-Child Policy", All-China Women's Federation, 23 April 2014, http://www.womenofchina.cn/html/womenofchina/report/172429-1.htm.

[19] Reggie Littlejohn of Women's Rights without Frontiers has responded negatively to media reports about an apparent relaxing of China's birth-control policy and continues to fight passionately for an end to coercive population control in China ("The One-Child Policy Has Not Been Relaxed", accessed 10 February 2017, http://www.womensrightswithoutfrontiers.org/index.php?nav=one_child_policy).

[20] "China Formally Eases One-Child Policy", BBC News, 28 December 2013, http://www.bbc.co.uk/news/world-asia-china-25533339.

[21] "A Change in Population Policy", Beijing Review, 8 May 2014, http://www.bjreview.com.cn/print/txt/2014-05/05/content_617101.htm.

[22] "Re-Education through Labor, One-Child Policy in China", Human Rights Watch, 17 November 2013, http://www.hrw.org/news/2013/11/17/watch-re-education-through-labor-one-child-policy-china.

approach to enforced birth control followed by the Chinese authorities, Yang Wenzhuang, the director-general of the Department of Community Family Planning under the National Health and Family Planning Commission, confirmed that the "family planning principle" had not changed and was merely being "fine tuned".[23]

Unwittingly, when the Western media broadcast the message that the policy is changing for the better without questioning the legitimacy of the policy itself, it bolsters the credibility of an inherently abusive system. Why should anyone who cares about women's liberty wish to praise a government for its benevolence in granting limited freedoms it had no right to curtail in the first place? Rather than allowing ourselves to be distracted by these acts of window dressing on the part of the Chinese authorities, attention needs to remain squarely focused on the injustice of the policy itself and on its wholly unacceptable treatment of women.

The necessity argument (insofar as it can be described as an argument) is more insidious in terms of both its persistence in the public consciousness and the implications for the status of women. The necessity argument is built upon the apocalyptic horror of overpopulation destroying the world, a fear that has its roots in the writing of the much-discredited Rev. Malthus over two hundred years ago. In his 1798 work *An Essay on the Principle of Population*, Malthus asserted: "Population, when unchecked, increases in a geometrical ratio. Subsistence increases only in an arithmetical ratio. A slight acquaintance with numbers will shew the immensity of the first power in

---

[23] "Most Chinese Provincial Areas Relax One-Child Policy", China Daily .com.cn, 10 July 2014, http://www.chinadaily.com.cn/china/2014-07/10 /content_17706811.htm.

comparison of the second."[24] This algorithm, asserted by Malthus as though it were a self-evident truth, was not the first expression of panic about overpopulation (population was a subject of concern in fifth-century Athens), but possibly because Malthus' argument is couched in quasi-mathematical terms, it has been undeservedly influential when it comes to the modern understanding of population and poverty.

A stronger reason why this long-debunked Malthusian logic continues to be so attractive to the ruling classes is that it blames the poor for their own poverty. The poor are hungry because they breed; they have the temerity to have children. It is infinitely easier to focus attention on eliminating the poor or at least explaining why it is all their fault for existing in the first place rather than to question the corruption and greed, the inequalities and injustices, which trap certain sectors of the population into lives of poverty in the first place.

Overpopulation is so firmly rooted in the public consciousness that it continues to be accepted without question, in spite of twentieth-century doomsayers such as Paul Ehrlich having been repeatedly disproved—sixty-five million Americans did not die of starvation during the eighties, India is doing quite well economically, Britain still very much exists as a nation and is not filled with hungry people, the stench of dead fish is rarely cited as a reason to evacuate coastal areas and the world's population has not been catastrophically depleted. Julian Simon, perhaps the most famous opponent of the overpopulation hysteria of the seventies, argued convincingly that humanity is a resource in itself. Central to his thesis was the argument that "human

---

[24] Thomas Malthus, *An Essay on the Principle of Population*, 1998, Electronic Scholarly Publishing Project, p. 4, http://www.esp.org/books/malthus/population/malthus.pdf.

beings are not just more mouths to feed, but are productive and inventive minds that help find creative solutions to man's problems, thus leaving us better off over the long run."[25] Three years before his death, Simon opined: "It is very frustrating that after twenty-five years of the anti-pessimists being proven entirely right, and the doomsayers being proven entirely wrong, their credibility and influence waxes ever greater."[26]

Arguments against the overpopulation status quo may finally have left the fringes where Julian Simon did intellectual battle forty years ago, but even with more academics challenging overpopulation and the human rights abuses justified in the name of "regulating population", neo-Malthusianism is proving to be a stubborn falsehood to dislodge.

The reality or even the possibility that false ideas about population growth have left an enduring legacy of human rights abuses and death ought by rights to have provoked some expression of remorse from overpopulation's most vociferous champions. Instead, Paul and Ann Ehrlich have responded to criticisms of their work *The Population Bomb* with an astonishing level of arrogance.[27] They continue to insist that their repeatedly debunked predictions were simply not dire enough, dismiss critics as "silly" without taking much trouble to explain why and assert their unshakeable pride in their work.[28]

---

[25] Quoted in Mark Skousen, *The Making of Modern Economics: The Lives and Ideas of the Great Thinkers* (New York: Routledge, 2016), p. 89. This much-cited statement by Julian Simon sums up—in one sentence—the central argument against population doomsayers such as Simon's chief opponent, Paul Ehrlich.

[26] Julian L. Simon, "Earth Day: Spiritually Uplifting, Intellectually Debased", 5 May 1995, http://www.juliansimon.com/writings/Articles/EARTHDA5.txt.

[27] Paul Ehrlich, *The Population Bomb* (New York: Ballantine Books, 1968).

[28] Paul R. Ehrlich and Anne H. Ehrlich, "The Population Bomb Revisited", *Electronic Journal of Sustainable Development* 1:3 (2009): 63–71, http://citeseerx .ist.psu.edu/viewdoc/download?doi=10.1.1.403.8993&rep=rep1&type=pdf.

The heartlessness at the centre of Malthusian thinking was satirised as early as the nineteenth century by Charles Dickens in *A Christmas Carol*. When the miserly Ebeneezer Scrooge is told by philanthropists that many poor people would rather die than go to the workhouse, the only place of shelter for the most destitute in Victorian England, he responds: "If they would rather die, they had better do it and decrease the surplus population."[29] There is a further reference to this in Thomas Hardy's darkest novel, *Jude the Obscure*, where a child kills his siblings then hangs himself, leaving behind the note to his parents "Because we are too menny."

The injustice of blaming the poor for existing belongs firmly in the past. However, rather than consign such outdated and disproven theories to the history books, these theories have simply been reapplied in recent years to the perceived overbreeding of ethnic rather than social groups. At the risk of being provocative, it could be said that population alarmists have switched from being racist snobs to being simply racists. One of the many claims used to vilify immigrants is that they "breed like rabbits" and will overrun the indigenous population because of their perceived higher birth rates (though the extent to which second-generation immigrants adopt family sizes akin to the local population is less well broadcast). The higher fertility rates in some parts of the developing world are likewise trumpeted as a sign of the ignorance of certain populations and the need for Western intervention to provide "modern family planning". When Prince William expressed his sincere concerns about population growth in developing countries and its impact on the environment—at precisely

---

[29] Charles Dickens, *A Christmas Carol* (Mineola, N.Y.: Dover Publications, 2014), p. 6.

the time his wife was carrying their third child—it did not apparently occur to him that his comments might come across as a little hypocritical. The distasteful image of a privileged white man fathering a third child whilst fretting about the number of Africans did not go entirely without comment in some areas of the British press.

Nigerian engineer Chinwuba Iyizoba made the telling observation in response to concerns expressed about Nigeria's growing population: "The real reason for poverty is corrupt rulers, not a lack of birth control."[30] He dismissed as "ignorance" the view that Nigeria's problems had anything to do with population, echoing a view held by other critics of the overpopulation position: "What Malthusians fail to take into consideration is the human spirit of enterprise. Necessity is the mother of invention. This was the case with the breakthrough of Norman Boulaug, the famous scientist who invented high yield crops. Even though Boulaug did not realize it, he had refuted Malthus."[31]

Millions of Chinese citizens did not starve during the Great Leap Forward because they were too numerous to be fed; China lost nearly 5 percent of its population due to a complex and deadly combination of politics, incompetence, corruption and poor decision making regarding the production and distribution of crops. The Chinese Communist Party, through the implementation of birth-control policies, has deflected attention away from its own responsibility for what may well have been the worst famine in human history, and the West has aided and abetted

[30] Chinwuba Iyizoba, "Where an Ageing Population Is Not a Problem", MercatorNet, 24 May 2011, http://www.mercatornet.com/articles/view /where_an_ageing_population_is_not_a_problem/.
[31] Ibid.

them in doing so. Rather than question how and why a vast country with enviable natural resources allowed millions to perish, international agencies have congratulated China for punishing the population for apparently breeding itself to destruction. Every time a UN department, international aid agency or government praises the one-child policy, defends or refuses to challenge it, the West colludes with China's suppression of women's rights and the ongoing denial about China's bloody past.

In the context of discussion about the status of women, the notion that coercive or forced population control is a "necessary evil" falls into the trap of treating women's lives as expendable in pursuit of some imagined greater good. The overwhelming majority of societies and cultures around the world abandoned the practice of human sacrifice centuries ago, but sacrificing women's lives in the name of conservation is little different to sacrificing virgins for the good of Mother Earth.

This is an issue of paramount importance to those who campaign for women's rights. It is an appalling atrocity against a woman's liberty and dignity to be forcibly aborted or sterilised, and China's decades' long war on women is the most crass example of the forcible suppression of childbearing anywhere in the world. The very fact that the expression "one-child policy" is used in political and media circles as a neutral term is evidence of the disregard shown towards the abuse of women who desire to be mothers. Few would refer in neutral terms to policies such as apartheid, segregation or the forcible separation from their families of children belonging to certain ethnic groups, though at the time, the same deafening silence prevailed. If the true horror faced by women in China for approaching forty years is to be taken seriously and brought to a definite end, it must first be confronted and spoken of as it really is, free of euphemism and political jargon.

It might be helpful for Westerners to consider whether they would feel as happy to explain away an enforced population-control policy if it occurred in their own country. How would a British or American couple feel if the registrar at their wedding greeted the happy event with a patronising lecture about the need to have an IUD fitted? How would a woman feel if she were expected to inform her manager every time she started her period, only to be instructed to take a pregnancy test and inform him of the result if she were a few days' late? How happy would a resident of San Francisco or London be to witness a neighbour having his house ransacked and vandalised because his wife won't submit to an abortion? How would any woman feel about being dragged to a hospital heavily pregnant, held down and forcibly sedated? If any of these prospects fill the reader with horror, the situation faced by millions of women in China for decades should feel no less appalling.

To dismiss China's disastrous population-control policy as "none of my business" is to deny Chinese women a place within the universal sisterhood feminists claim to believe in, perhaps because of a residual embarrassment that women sometimes suffer because they want to have children. It is worth considering whether the reason for the West's virtual silence on the subject of forced abortion in China is any different from the silence which greets forced abortion under any circumstances in any country, or the silence which greets sex-selective abortion or botched abortions carried out in "safe, legal" facilities. Chinese women may have been left to their fate because the weapons that have been used to oppress them are contraception and abortion, the two sacred relics of

feminism before which all women are supposed to bow
down and worship.

When Ehrlich's work *The Population Bomb* was published, it was an international best seller and was greeted
with accolades across the globe. As has already been discussed, Ehrlich's predictions did not turn out to be correct. In 1968, another tract was published which provoked
widespread condemnation, anger and disbelief around the
world. The author of that work predicted:

> Who will blame a government which in its attempt to
> resolve the problems affecting an entire country resorts
> to the same measures as are regarded as lawful by mar-
> ried people in the solution of a particular family diffi-
> culty? Who will prevent public authorities from favoring
> those contraceptive methods which they consider more
> effective? Should they regard this as necessary, they may
> even impose their use on everyone. It could well hap-
> pen, therefore, that when people, either individually or
> in family or social life, experience the inherent difficulties
> of the divine law and are determined to avoid them, they
> may give into the hands of public authorities the power to
> intervene in the most personal and intimate responsibility
> of husband and wife.[32]

As millions of women in China know to their cost, that
prediction came to pass just eleven years after *Humanae
Vitae* was published.

---

[32] Paul VI, encyclical letter *Humanae Vitae* (25 July 1968), no. 17, http://
w2.vatican.va/content/paul-vi/en/encyclicals/documents/hf_p-vi_enc
_25071968_humanae-vitae.html.

Outsourcing Reproduction: ART, Surrogacy and the Commodification of the Female Body

Parents do not own their children, although this view has a surprisingly long and respectable intellectual history. Aristotle, for instance, thought that children belonged to their parents as a product belongs to a producer or even—like a tooth or hair—as a part of them. But although such views cast a long shadow over current thinking about parenthood, we no longer do or should think of children as chattels to be disposed of as parents think fit.

—David Archard

Assisted reproductive technology (ART) has always been portrayed as very much on the side of women, liberating women from the heartache of infertility or the slavery of their own biological clocks. In vitro fertilisation (IVF) is sometimes described as the ideal way to postpone motherhood and cap a successful career with a child when the woman—not her body—wishes. As with abortion, ART promotes (unwittingly perhaps) the idea that the female body is in some ways independent of a woman's identity and can be said to be pitted against her either by refusing to produce offspring at the desired time (or at all) or by insisting upon

David Archard, "Children Are Not Products", *Guardian*, 31 July 2006, http://www.theguardian.com/commentisfree/2006/aug/01/comment.schools.

remaining fecund in defiance of a woman's lifestyle choices. Like abortion, ART is presented as protecting women from the dictates of their own bodies and providing them with a necessary tool in the battle for empowerment.

It therefore caused some consternation in Britain when celebrated feminist Germaine Greer attacked the fertility industry for exploiting women. She said:

> Sometimes I think that really the problem is the concept of motherhood, which we can't give any real structure to. We now have a "genetic" mother, who supplies eggs. It depends entirely on where she is if she is going to be allowed to know what happens to the eggs. And women tend to care. An egg is not a sperm, we do not produce 400 million of them in one go. One miserable little egg pops every month. Then they give you follicle stimulating hormones and you have seventeen or something [eggs] and they give you cut price IVF and distribute the rest of your eggs where they see fit.... I'm sorry. Did we talk about this? Did we sit down and talk about what eggs mean to women? The whole discourse has been distorted from the beginning by the fertility industry.... I've got a suspicion, which I need to investigate properly, that we got legalised abortion precisely because the fertility indus-try needed it.... They were the ones who wanted to be able to terminate pregnancies and manipulate the products of conception at will.

Greer went on to suggest that David Steel, the politician responsible for the legalisation of abortion in Britain, was merely a puppet of the fertility barons.[1]

---

[1] Jemma Buckley, "Germaine Greer Slams Elton John Because His Hus-band David Furnish Is Named as 'Mother' on Birth Certificates of Their Two Sons", *Daily Mail*, updated 25 May 2015, http://www.dailymail.co.uk/news /article-3095268/Germaine-Greer-slams-Elton-John-husband-David-Furnish -named-mother-birth-certificates-two-sons.html#ixzz3bGbfbwPn.

It is interesting to note that after decades of denigrating motherhood as a form of slavery, some radical feminists appear to be fighting to reclaim motherhood from an industry that has done far more in terms of denigrating motherhood than feminism ever did and is in danger of rendering it obsolete.

For the sake of clarity, I should note at this point that I use the terms "egg donation" and "egg donor" for want of more accurate terminology. In reality—and Greer's comments hint heavily at this—the giving away of human gametes cannot be placed in the same category as blood donation, for example, or becoming a kidney donor. To donate egg or sperm for the purposes of creating a human embryo is to become the biological parent of a human life; it involves the creation of a biological connection that involves both serious responsibilities and potentially serious consequences for both parties and for society more broadly.

Greer's intervention should not have caused quite such surprise, as the fertility industry's denigration of women is written into the misogynist terminology used to describe the procedures and women's contributions specifically. An egg donor is referred to as a "genetic contributor" when the more accurate term is surely "mother", and a surrogate becomes a "gestational carrier", a term more reminiscent of an incubator than a pregnant woman. Even more telling is the failure of the two most commonly used terms, IVF and ART, to even mention the woman. As anthropologist Sarah Franklin notes,[2] the term IVF refers to the one part of the process which occurs outside the woman's body. The fact that virtually the entire nine months' gestation of an IVF baby occurs in utero is not in evidence in the title,

---

[2] Karen Throsby, "'Calling It a Day': The Decision to End IVF Treatment" (PhD thesis, Gender Institute, London School of Economics, April 2002), http://etheses.lse.ac.uk/110/1/Throsby_Calling_it_a_day.pdf.

nor indeed in the colloquial term "test tube baby" with its images of babies growing and developing in a jar. It is tempting to ask, what's in a name? but the answer is a great deal when a procedure that puts such a severe strain on a woman's body fails to acknowledge her existence.

Feminist voices have been raised against certain aspects of ART for many years, long before Greer's interview. When the cloning debate was raging at the time of the millennium, some feminists pointed out that if cloning ever became a common practice within scientific research, it would require millions of human eggs for which women would effectively be the battery hens. Besides the misuse and degradation of both human eggs and women's bodies that would be involved in such an endeavour, there were significant safety risks to consider.

Beyond the media hype, there were always serious questions as to whether human cloning could ever become a common practice in scientific research, but even when research repeatedly fails to achieve its stated aims, women may still pay a price. When South Korea's idolised scientist Hwang Woo-Suk was exposed as a fraud, a little-discussed fact was that his futile experiments in human embryo cloning involved 2,061 eggs taken from 169 women:[3] 169 women had their bodies pillaged in the name of research amid concerns that female members of Hwang Woo-Suk's lab had donated their own eggs in violation of accepted ethical standards.[4]

[3] Katrina George, "Women Don't Need to Risk Their Health with Egg Donation", *Age*, 18 November 2009, http://www.theage.com.au/opinion /contributors/women-dont-need-to-risk-their-health-with-egg-donation -20091118-il8l.html.

[4] "The Cloning Scandal of Hwang Woo-Suk", Stem Cells: Biology, Bioethics, and Applications, accessed 7 March 2018, http://stemcell bioethics .wikischolars.columbia.edu/The+Cloning+Scandal+of+Hwang+Woo-Suk.

A detail of the debate that was almost overlooked once the furore over cloning had subsided was that egg harvesting and/or donation forms a necessary part of IVF procedures practised in fertility clinics around the world. Since the procedure is the same, so too are the safety risks in principle, though clinics may perhaps be even more cavalier with egg donors than with infertile patients in terms of numbers of eggs sought for use. Those risks are carried solely by women.

In IVF, the man's contribution invariably involves masturbating into a container with the assistance of pornographic materials that objectify and degrade women—even the male act in IVF is antiwoman—while women bear the brunt of the entire ordeal: drugs with unpleasant and sometimes dangerous side effects to stop normal menstruation, more drugs to stimulate multiple ovulation, a surgical procedure to extract the mature eggs and, when she goes through the process for her own benefit, the very real possibility of not giving birth to a baby, even after several cycles.

A documentary made in the United States entitled *Eggsploitation* uncovered what it calls "the infertility industry's dirty little secret", giving a voice to women whose health has been seriously compromised by egg donation.[5] They include a woman who suffered a stroke as a result of the hormone injections, a PhD student who experienced massive internal bleeding when a doctor nicked an artery during the egg-harvesting process and a student called Alexandra who lost an ovary due to complications and was diagnosed with breast cancer in her early thirties.

The documentary raises the question as to how a purportedly pro-woman industry can have been in existence

---

[5] *Eggsploitation* (video), directed by Justin Baird and Jennifer Lahl, written by Jennifer Lahl and Evan Rosa, Center for Bioethics and Culture, 9 August 2010.

for over thirty years and shown such reluctance to inves-
tigate the long-term health risks faced by the very women
who frequent these clinics and provide gametes for infertile couples. An article in the scientific journal *Nature* in
2006 warned about serious concerns among some doctors
about the long-term health risks, particularly an increase in
some cancers (breast, ovarian, uterine) among women who
undergo egg harvesting and IVF. The article acknowledged the uncertainty and lack of available data, but also
the unwillingness of some doctors to register negative out-
comes and the vested interest IVF practitioners have in
failing to support longitudinal studies, stating that "private
fertility clinics may have little interest in finding out the
potential risks of the drugs they use."[6] Those who glibly
talk about the rights of women to sovereignty over their
own bodies should surely be calling the fertility industry
to account for its callous disregard for women's health and
its failure to allow women a fully informed choice before
undergoing these procedures.

As an article in the *New York Times* stated: "We rarely
hear from the other side, former patients who, in refusing to give up, endured addictive, debilitating and trau-
matizing cycles. Those contemplating treatments have a
right to know about the health risks, ethical concerns,
broken marriages and, for many, deep depression often
associated with failed treatments. They need objective,
independent advice from health care and mental health
professionals focused on the person's well-being instead
of the profit."[7]

---

[6] Helen Pearson, "Health Effects of Egg Donation May Take Decades to
Emerge", *Nature*, 10 August 2006, http://www.nature.com/nature/journal
/v442/n7103/full/442607a.html.

[7] Miriam Zoll and Pamela Tsigdinos, "Selling the Fantasy of Fertility",
New York Times, 11 September 2013, http://www.nytimes.com/2013/09/12
/opinion/selling-the-fantasy-of-fertility.html?partner=rss&emc=rss&_r=0.

Surrogacy and Serfdom

The international register *Find a Surrogate* contains the names of donors from all over the world, with India providing the highest number of registered egg donors by a wide margin.[8] Almost inevitably, if a country has a booming surrogacy industry, egg donation will not come far behind, and though the medical, legal and ethical problems associated with egg donation are identical in many countries, the health risks faced by those who actively participate in IVF may be greater in developing countries. When medical complications arise as a result of the invasive egg-harvesting process, a donor in a country with poor infrastructures may struggle to access affordable medical assistance in a timely manner. Moreover, as with surrogates, it is unclear what, if any, information these women are being given about the potential health risks. An investigation by the newspaper *Indian Express* interviewed doctors who dismissed as a myth the idea that egg donors are predominantly poor and uneducated. At the same time, the donors themselves spoke of the financial incentives to sell their eggs, believed there to be "no risks" involved and had never heard of serious complications such as ovarian hyperstimulation.

A study of egg donation and fertility tourism published by the journal *Cultural Politics* details the cases of two women, Alina and Raluca, which were reported in the European Parliament in 2005. Both were poor factory workers from Bucharest who had had little formal education and did not understand the complexities of egg donation. They both suffered debilitating complications following egg donation, and Alina had a history of serious

[8] Pritha Chatterjee and Mayura Janwalkar, "The Great Indian Egg Bazaar", *Indian Express*, 9 February 2014, http://indianexpress.com/article/india/india-others/the-great-indian-egg-bazaar/.

medical problems which any reputable doctor should have accepted made her unsuited to being a donor.[9] In a separate case, an Israeli donor (cited in a 2009 report) was reportedly told by a doctor that egg donation was as simple and painless as blood donation.[10]

Fertility tourism is a burgeoning industry in many developing countries, including famously India, where the Law Commission has described it as a "gold pot", through which "wombs in India are on rent, which translates into babies for foreigners and dollars for Indian surrogate mothers."[11] In October 2015, the Indian government finally banned foreign couples from using Indian clinics,[12] a move that pitted it against a powerful industry which has facilitated the desires of wealthy Western couples for years[13] in that it offered relatively low costs (around a third of the cost of surrogacy in the United States[14]) and the absence of many of the restrictions found in other countries.[15]

---

[9] Susanne Lundin, " 'I Want a Baby; Don't Stop Me from Being a Mother': An Ethnographic Study on Fertility Tourism and Egg Trade", *Cultural Politics* 8, no. 2 (2012), http://culturalpolitics.dukejournals.org/content/8/2/327.full .pdf+html.

[10] Ibid.

[11] Law Commission of India, Report No. 228 (August 2009), http://law commissionofindia.nic.in/reports/report228.pdf.

[12] Grhari, "Indian Government Hurriedly Notifies Stopping of Surrogacy for Foreign Nationals", Web-Blog of Indian Surrogacy Law Centre, 28 October 2015, http://blog.indiansurrogacylaw.com/indian-government-hurriedly -notifies-stopping-of-surrogacy-for-foreign-national/.

[13] Sarojini N, "Reproductive Tourism in India: Issues and Challenges", Sama Resource Group for Women & Health, 8 November 2012, http:// www.med.uio.no/helsam/english/research/global-governance-health/news /sarojini-reproductive-tourism-2012(1).pdf.

[14] Neeta Lal, "Pitfalls of Surrogacy in India Exposed", *Asia Times*, 24 May 2012, http://www.atimes.com/atimes/South_Asia/NE24Df02.html.

[15] Sreeja Jaiswal, "Commercial Surrogacy in India: An Ethical Assessment of Existing Legal Scenario from the Perspective of Women's Autonomy and Reproductive Rights", *Gender, Technology and Development* 16, no. 1 (2012): 1–28, http://gtd.sagepub.com/content/16/1/1.full.pdf.

Commercial surrogacy involves a couple, the "commissioning parents" paying a fee to a clinic which will then pay a local woman to be this couple's surrogate. The majority of surrogates in India and other developing countries live in poverty; they may be expected to sign contracts they cannot read, in a language they do not understand, and agree to procedures they have never heard of and that are rarely explained to them. Typically (though not exclusively), the woman will reside in dormitory-style housing during her pregnancy, separated from her family, where she will receive medical care and be kept under close observation. After the birth, the baby will be handed over to the commissioning parents and the woman paid a fee.

Fertility tourism is lauded within some areas of the Western media as a mutually beneficial system in which poor women earn a significant sum of money and childless couples get their dream baby. However, fertility tourism is exploitative on a number of levels. First and foremost, perhaps, it builds upon a residual colonial mentality that sees women from developing countries as gratefully subservient to the needs of wealthy Westerners. There is an unwritten assumption in many of these transactions that the woman on the receiving end is grateful for the chance to be impregnated with someone else's child, with the Western couple taking on the role of the benevolent colonial master, temporarily adopting a poor woman then walking away with the child she carried for nine months in her own body and quite possibly having nothing further to do with her.

Outsourcing reproduction in this way represents a form of legalised serfdom of women, a colonisation of the female body through the purchase and control of women's fertility that is regarded as entirely unacceptable in many of the countries in which commissioning parents reside. It is not without reason that countries such as Britain, Canada and

Australia ban commercial surrogacy and others such as Italy, France and Germany ban surrogacy altogether.[16] In France in 1991, the highest court in the land ruled that "the human body is not lent out, is not rented out, and is not sold."[17] That ruling recognised the inherently degrading nature of surrogacy of all kinds.

An argument used against such a position, particularly in feminist circles—though feminism is divided on the subject of commercial surrogacy—is that a woman has absolute sovereignty over her own body, an echo of the position laid out by John Stuart Mill: "Over himself, over his own body and mind, the individual is sovereign."[18] Therefore, a woman may do with her body whatever she wishes, even if that includes renting, lending or selling it. To prohibit her from using her body as she wishes is said to be to fall into the patriarchal trap of attacking a woman's liberty in the most intimate area of her life—the perimeters of her own physical existence.

However, this position is based upon a failure to understand a fundamental principle of human rights: that is, that basic human rights are both inviolable and *inalienable*—a necessary paradox of human rights is that an individual cannot be separated from his fundamental human rights whether or not he chooses to be so. If this were not the case, it would be a comparatively small step from a person choosing, for whatever reason, to sell himself into

[16] "Surrogacy as an Infertility Treatment", Fertility Treatment Abroad, accessed 11 February 2017, http://fertility.treatmentabroad.com/treatments/surrogacy.

[17] "Surrogacy Contracts", Surrogate Motherhood in India, Stanford University, 2008, https://www.stanford.edu/group/womenscourage/Surrogacy/surrogacy_contracts.html.

[18] John Stuart Hill, *On Liberty* (London: Longman, Roberts, and Green, 1859), chap. 1, Introductory, 1.9, http://www.econlib.org/library/Mill/mlLbty1.html.

slavery, and a more vulnerable individual being coerced into doing so. More fundamentally, however, the human body is not property; a person cannot therefore be said to be owned, even by himself, without becoming an object of transaction.

Female empowerment is very much a buzzword of contemporary political debate, and for that reason, the allegedly pro-woman characteristics of international surrogacy are emphasised in media reports. A report in the British newspaper *The Daily Telegraph*,[19] for example, described a clinic in India run by a certain Dr Nayna Patel, who was portrayed as a feminist and, by one commissioning parent, as "an absolute saint". A great deal of attention was given to her work with the surrogates, to teach them embroidery and her insistence that they keep control of the money they earn. The fact that Dr Patel herself described her work as "a baby-making factory" apparently did little to tarnish her pro-woman image.

The feel-good stories make for compelling reading. It is difficult not to want to rejoice with the infertile couples decorating the nursery in anticipation of a longed-for child who will shortly be born on their behalf. However, beyond these sanitised news features, it is very hard to build a coherent argument in favour of fertility tourism or any form of commercial surrogacy from the perspective of women's empowerment.

From the moment a woman in a developing country becomes a surrogate, she renders herself vulnerable legally, physically and emotionally. Current guidelines by India's Medical Council allow up to three embryos to be

[19] Tom Rowley, "The British Babies Made in India", *Telegraph*, 21 September 2013, http://www.telegraph.co.uk/women/womens-health/10324970/The-British-babies-made-in-India.html.

implanted into a surrogate[20] when, as B. L. Chaudhary states in his paper "Assisted Reproductive Techniques: Ethical and Legal Issues", "in Britain, the maximum is two and many European countries are moving towards a single embryo implant."[21] There are sound medical reasons for avoiding multiple embryo transfer as multiple pregnancies can increase the risk of miscarriage, premature delivery, stillbirth and a raft of other complications for women.

Not only can a surrogate be the subject of multiple embryo transfer, without her consent or even her knowledge; a commissioning couple can demand that a surrogate mother undergo so-called "foetal reduction", otherwise known as selective abortion,[22] with the surrogate having little power to resist such a demand even if it goes against her principles. There have also been allegations that surrogates have been instructed to take abortion pills by clinic doctors without being told what the pills were for and being then told that they had suffered a miscarriage.[23]

---

[20] Guidelines for ART Clinics in India, chap. 3, "Code of Practice, Ethical Considerations and Legal Issues", ICMR/NAMS, accessed 7 March 2018, http://icmr.nic.in/art/Chapter_3.pdf.

[21] B. L. Chaudhary, "Assisted Reproductive Techniques: Ethical and Legal Issues", J Indian Acad Forensic Med 34, no. 4 (October–December 2012): 352, http://medind.nic.in/jal/t12/i4/jalt12i4p350.pdf.

[22] Sama-Resource Group for Woman and Health, Birthing A Market: A Study on Commercial Surrogacy (New Delhi: Sama-Resource Group for Woman and Health, 2012), p. 65, http://www.academia.edu/7885788/Birthing_A _Market_A_Study_on_Commercial_Surrogacy_Sama_Resource_Group_for _Women_and_Health.

[23] Himanshi Dhawan, "Unregulated Surrogacy Industry Worth over $2bn Thrives without Legal Framework", Times of India, 18 July 2013, http:// timesofindia.indiatimes.com/india/Unregulated-surrogacy-industry-worth -over-2bn-thrives-without-legal-framework/articleshow/21131823.cms. These issues do not only arise when surrogacy occurs in developing countries. There have been a number of stories in the Western press in recent years, involving surrogates with multiple pregnancies, resisting pressure to

As the death of one surrogate in 2012 revealed, the physical well-being of a surrogate may be sacrificed in favour of the baby if a couple have paid money for that child. Thirty-year-old Premila Vaghela was carrying a child for an American couple when she collapsed during her eighth month. The baby boy was successfully delivered by caesarean section, but the mother died. The *Times of India* report could not quite avoid a hint of bitterness: "On Wednesday, Premila, who was eight months pregnant, died due to unexplained complications. But she completed her job—the child was delivered and is in the NICU recuperating from early birth."[24] Premila's death was barely reported outside her own country, perhaps because it drew too much attention to the risks facing surrogate mothers, but also to the bizarre mirror image of abortion rhetoric that commercial surrogacy has created. Both abortion and commercial surrogacy render it necessary for one of the two human lives involved in pregnancy to become expendable in certain situations—the baby or the surrogate mother—creating an unsustainable ethical paradox which feminists of all political persuasions need to confront but instead choose to ignore. There was no international coverage of Premila's death, no outraged articles in progressive broadsheets, no candlelit vigils outside embassies, no banners raised, no emotive press releases issued by civil rights groups. One might almost be left with the impression that the deaths of economically

---

abort one of the babies. See Carl Campanile, "Surrogate Defies Birth Parents' Abortion Demand", *New York Post*, 14 December 2015, https://nypost.com/2015/12/14/surrogate-defying-birth-parents-abortion-demand/.

[24] "Surrogate Mother Dies of Complications", *Times of India*, 17 May 2012, http://timesofindia.indiatimes.com/city/ahmedabad/Surrogate-mother-dies-of-complications/articleshow/13181592.cms.

disadvantaged women only matter if their deaths are ideologically useful.

A surrogacy clinic has a vested interest in monitoring
a surrogate's health while pregnant, but postpartum, the
woman's health may be of little consequence, and it is quite
often in the days and weeks following birth that complications such as sepsis can occur. Nor is a clinic responsible
for the surrogate's mental and emotional health following
the birth, and there is no way of knowing how many surrogates go on to develop postnatal depression and other
trauma responses following the loss of the child.

Clinics such as Dr Patel's may insist upon the woman
retaining control of the money she earns as a surrogate,
but there is no legal requirement for a clinic to protect a
woman's financial interests, leaving the door wide open
for women to be financially exploited. There is little to
prevent a woman from being forced by her husband or
another family member to rent out her body (possibly
repeatedly) for financial reasons, and it is highly unlikely
that a surrogate in a developing country would have
recourse to legal assistance if she is cheated or mistreated in
any way by her agency.

Beyond the financial concerns, there is a notable lack
within commercial surrogacy of any acknowledgement of
the surrogate mother's basic human rights. In Britain, as in
many jurisdictions, a surrogate mother is presumed to be
the birth mother even if the baby is not genetically linked
to her, and an adoption process is necessary for the intended
mother to claim the child:[25] Section 27(1) of the Human
Fertilisation and Embryology Act 1990 cites the surrogate as the child's birth mother, thereby acknowledging

---

[25] "Legal Issues around Surrogacy", Human Fertilisation & Embryology
Authority, last updated 22 October 2013, http://www.hfea.gov.uk/1424.html.

the symbiotic relationship between the pregnant woman and the baby she carries. In India, a surrogate has no right to refuse to give up the baby if she bonds with it during the course of the pregnancy. Commissioning parents are presumed to be the legal parents of the child with the surrogate maintaining her subservient position as a mere gestational carrier. Both the surrogate mother and her spouse must relinquish all rights to the child.[26]

It is impossible to calculate the heartache faced by a woman who carries a baby in her womb for nine months and then has to come to terms with being parted from that child forever. India's Assisted Reproductive Technologies (Regulation) Bill, like the guidelines that preceded it, makes some attempt at addressing the possibility that a surrogate may form an attachment to the child she carries, and a surrogate under the terms of the bill is not permitted to carry a child to which she is genetically linked; that is, she cannot also provide the egg fertilised to create the baby she gestates.[27] However, this demonstrates a failure to grasp the emotional complexities surrounding the symbiotic mother–child relationship that develops during pregnancy. Genetic connections may well cause the mother to feel a more powerful connection with the child who will then be her biological child in every way, including genetics—but there is surely more to the mother–child relationship than genetics?

An unintentionally heartbreaking account of a surrogate mother being parted from her babies can be found

[26] "The Assisted Reproductive Technologies (Regulation) Bill" (2010), Ministry of Health and Family Welfare, Government of India, New Delhi, http://icmr.nic.in/guide/ART%20REGULATION%20Draft%20Bill1.pdf.

[27] Ibid.; *Guidelines for ART Clinics in India*, chap. 3, "Code of Practice, Ethical Considerations and Legal Issues", ICMR/NAMS, http://icmr.nic.in/art/Chapter_3.pdf.

in an upbeat story in a British newspaper about a gay couple who had twins through a surrogacy arrangement. The article very much emphasises how much the couple want the children and their alleged victimhood as "hotel prisoners" when one of them is forced to stay in India with the twins to iron out legal difficulties. However, when describing the moment he claimed the twins, "Steve" said of the surrogate: "Her English wasn't very great, but she was perhaps a little bit too attached and there was a little bit of an awkward time when it came to handing the babies over and for her to say goodbye. She was reminded that it was a deal and she was fine. She was quite tender with them because they are cute and they are twins. But the reminder to her by me and the carer was a simple pointer that it was a deal and the time had come for her to say goodbye to them. I understood her attachment to them, but it was going too far and she needed to be reminded."[28]

No effort is made to disguise the language of transaction: "It was a deal." He uses the word "deal" twice in quick succession. A woman is struggling to come to terms with being parted from babies she might well regard as hers, and the man's major concern is not her welfare but reminding her to keep up her side of the deal. Another disturbing detail is the condescending, slightly threatening way in which the man asserts his mastery over the woman; he permits her as much attachment as he deems to be natural, but feels the need to "remind" her that the twins are his property not hers. This story caused considerable

[28] Shekhar Bhatia, "Indian Surrogacy Industry: We Could Never Have Imagined We'd Be Parents", *Telegraph*, 26 May 2012, http://www.telegraph.co.uk/health/healthnews/9292553/Indian-surrogacy-industry-we-could-never-have-imagined-wed-be-parents.html.

comment when it first appeared, but the male, capitalist domination of a woman from a developing country was treated as a mere detail.

The attempts to close down fertility tourism in India and countries such as Thailand in the wake of the Baby Gammy scandal—in which an Australian couple left one of their twins with the Thai surrogate because he had Down's syndrome and other health problems—is necessary and welcome. However, media reports indicate that wealthy Westerners will keep finding new fertility markets to exploit whenever one closes, with Mexico and Cambodia being the latest destinations of choice.[29]

The many pitfalls of turning human reproduction into a multibillion dollar industry require a series of books to explore in any detail, but fundamentally, these ethical concerns are all indicators of a much more deeply rooted problem, and that is that the single biggest facilitator of female exploitation is poverty. It is certainly true that poverty causes women—and men for that matter—to be exploited in all kinds of ways, from organ selling to working for a pittance in sweatshops, but in the West, there are no celebrations of these forms of exploitation or any pretence that they are forms of empowerment in disguise. On the contrary, there is increasing public unease about the human cost of Western commercialism.

If more strenuous efforts were channelled into providing women with ways to escape the poverty trap—access to education, equality in the labour market, financial independence—the prospect of becoming yet another of

---

[29] Lindsay Murdoch, "'Somebody Has to Be the Icebreaker': Aussies Seeking Babies Turn to Cambodia", *Sydney Morning Herald*, 30 October 2015, http://www.smh.com.au/world/somebody-has-to-be-the-icebreaker-aussies-seeking-babies-turn-to-cambodia-20151027-gkjfj5.html#ixzz3qMBjMidJ.

the international surrogacy industry's poor players would be less tempting.

Rights of the Child

No ethical discussion of surrogacy or any form of ART can avoid asking serious questions about the rights of the child and the consequences for a baby severed after birth from the woman who bore him. Can a child be said to have the right to be nurtured and raised by his birth mother? Surrogates tend to be discouraged or, in some countries, prevented from breastfeeding to avoid bonding with the baby—does a baby have a right to be breastfed? In an era where it is recognised that breastfeeding benefits a growing baby's health and well-being, where corporations who discourage breastfeeding for commercial gain face international boycotts, is it really justifiable to separate a child from his nurturer in this preplanned way? Is breastfeeding yet another detail in a child's development that can be circumvented or ignored as irrelevant?

Concerns have been raised for decades about the potential psychological consequences for children separated from their birth mothers through adoption, and during the last thirty years, about the possible impact upon donor-conceived children who cannot trace their genetic mother or father. However, the significance of the gestational link specifically should not be underestimated[30] when we consider the wealth of research available on prenatal

---

[30] Susan Golombok et al., "Children Born through Reproductive Donation: A Longitudinal Study of Psychological Adjustment", *Journal of Child Psychology and Psychiatry, and Allied Disciplines* 54, no. 6 (2013): 653–60, http://www.ncbi.nlm.nih.gov/pmc/articles/PMC3586757/.

development and the impact of the pregnant woman's lifestyle and well-being upon the development of the unborn child. The fact that pregnancy is biologically and psychologically a preparation for the birth and rearing of the child is evidenced[31] through details such as the hormone changes the pregnant woman goes through, particularly the production of oxytocin or the "bonding" hormone released during labour. A pregnant woman and baby are predisposed to bond even where there is no genetic link, and careful consideration needs to be given to the long-term consequences of deliberately severing that gestational link between woman and child.

Children created through ART are portrayed in the media as blessed—what child could doubt its wantedness when so much time and money has been invested in bringing about its existence? However, this is very much a materialistic perspective on what it means for a human being to have value. When a child becomes a commodity, that child's happiness, safety and indeed its very identity become entirely dependent upon its wantedness.

The commonest moral objection to commercial surrogacy is that the child is treated as a commodity and given a price tag no matter how good the intentions behind the process might be. Indeed, Chaudhary goes so far as to compare the plight of a child produced through commercial surrogacy with "selling or trafficking of human beings".[32]

The link between trafficking and surrogacy may be much closer than international commentators are willing

---

[31] Linda Palmer, "Bonding Matters ... The Chemistry of Attachment", BabyReference.com, 6 August 2013, reprinted from *Attachment Parenting International News* 5, no. 2 (2002), http://babyreference.com/bonding-matters-the-chemistry-of-attachment/.

[32] Chaudhary, "Assisted Reproductive Techniques", 352.

to admit. A paper published in the *Australian Journal of Adoption* draws attention to the widely reported case of an Israeli man with convictions for sex offences involving children, who was able to gain legal rights over a girl through a surrogacy arrangement in India. The Israeli authorities were eventually alerted anonymously, but if it had not been for that tip-off, that child would have been placed directly into the hands of a sex offender.[33] This is not an isolated incident. When the Baby Gammy scandal made international headlines, it emerged that the abandoned baby's father had a string of convictions for sex offences against children, causing the Thai surrogate to demand the return of the twin the couple had taken home with them because she feared for the little girl's safety.[34]

In the 2015 *Vice* for HBO documentary *Outsourcing Embryos*, investigative journalist Gianna Toboni exposed India's black market in Caucasian babies conceived through surrogacy who were either never claimed by commissioning parents or were born without the knowledge of the commissioning parents; that is, multiple embryos were implanted into the surrogate, and the commissioning parents took home one baby, not knowing that the surrogate had given birth to twins. At one point in the documentary Toboni discussed with traffickers the possibility of buying a baby and was offered one on the spot.

When legal disputes arise surrounding a child conceived through ART, which they inevitably do in some

---

[33] "Israeli Horror as Sex Abuser Adopts Girl, 4", *Jewish Chronicle*, 6 June 2013, https://www.thejc.com/news/israel/israeli-horror-as-sex-abuser-adopts-girl-4-1.45624.

[34] Bridie Jabour and Brendan Foster, "Child Abuse Convictions of Gammy's Father Prompt Investigation", *Guardian*, 5 August 2014, http://www.theguardian.com/world/2014/aug/05/gammy-father-child-abuse-convictions-investigation.

cases, a child caught in the middle can find himself parentless and stateless.[35] Baby Manji was born as a result of a surrogacy agreement between a Japanese couple (the Yamadas) and an Indian surrogacy clinic. An IVF embryo was created, using Mr Yamada's sperm and an egg from an anonymous donor, then implanted into the womb of an Indian surrogate. The Yamadas divorced and Mrs Yamada expressed no wish to raise the child. Baby Manji was therefore left with three mothers—the commissioning mother, the surrogate mother and the egg donor—and at the same time, no mother. The commissioning mother was not genetically linked with the child, and both donor and surrogate had signed away their legal rights to the child. A child conceived through ART can have up to five parents—commissioning parents, gamete donors and surrogate—and also none. Beyond the horror of a child having no legal parents, a baby born as a result of international fertility treatment can also find himself stateless. Article 7 of the UN Convention on the Rights of the Child declares: "The child shall be registered immediately after birth and shall have the right from birth to a name, the right to acquire a nationality and. [sic] as far as possible, the right to know and be cared for by his or her parents."[36] But if we no longer have any reasonable idea of what constitutes a parent, how can we ensure that a child is raised by his parents? If a child has no legal mother, can he have a nationality?

[35] Kari Points, "Commercial Surrogacy and Fertility Tourism in India: The Case of Baby Manji", Kenan Institute for Ethics, Duke University, accessed 11 February 2017, https://web.duke.edu/kenanethics/CaseStudies/BabyManji .pdf.

[36] "Convention on the Rights of the Child", United Nations, Human Rights, Office of the High Commissioner, 20 November 1989, http://www .ohchr.org/en/professionalinterest/pages/crc.aspx.

The fertility industry is throwing up questions no one could have envisaged thirty years ago when Assisted Reproductive Technology became a reality—questions about the nature of human fertility, both its limitations and its purpose within society, but also questions which strike at the heart of what it means to be human: What is sexuality? What do we really mean by sexual and reproductive freedom? What is a mother? What is a father? If a woman's reproductive system can be disabled, suppressed, pillaged, rented out or sold to the highest bidder, if a baby can be first placed artificially into her womb and then given into the hands of strangers once gestation is complete, one must also surely ask, what is a child? What is a family? Are the primordial relationships between husband and wife, mother and child or indeed father and child, so irrelevant that they can be circumvented in this way?

The idea that children are the chattels of their parents is an ancient one that has been used to justify many abuses of children across the centuries. The idea of children having the legal and social status of slaves or even inanimate objects is jarring in an age where the assertion that children have rights separate from those of their parents is strongly made and even at times overemphasised; the acknowledgement of children's rights has been central to legislative efforts to protect children from violence and to ensure that children have access to education, healthcare, shelter and the accommodation of their basic needs, whatever these are thought to include.

The suggestion, therefore, that identifying children as the property of their parents is the conceptual cornerstone at which ART and abortion meet is likely to be met with howls of protest. Outwardly, the difference between abortion and ART appears massive, the one procedure destroying life, the other creating it, and it is in many ways harder to argue against ART than abortion for exactly that reason. There is still a residual sense of shame surrounding abortion, a belief however little articulated that abortion should not happen. Few women speak positively about their abortions or choose to speak of them at all, but by contrast, ART is spoken of positively and openly with little in the way of opposition.

The many ethical pitfalls surrounding ART are hidden behind a wall of euphemism and emotive argument that distracts attention from the harsh reality of an industry that has led to the destruction of millions of human embryos and incalculable heartache for thousands of couples. As soon as the creation of human life becomes the subject of legislation and commercial transaction, it becomes a commodity, whether or not the individual players intend this to be the case. When couples speak of a "right to a baby", they are unwittingly asserting a degree of ownership and an expectation that any life created on their behalf will fulfil their needs and desires. Once it has been accepted that couples (or indeed, single adults) have a right to become parents by any means necessary, it is a relatively short step to accepting a right not to be parents, depending upon the individual's lifestyle choices, particularly if one considers that embracing ART standardly necessitates accepting the destruction of human life in its early stages as part of the process.

ART and abortion perpetuate the otherwise discredited myth that children are the property of their parents and can be created or disposed of according to the needs and desires of others. That this is an unfashionable and controversial statement is without question, but for the sake of future generations, there must be a way forward that is both compassionate to the childless and truthful about the moral, biological and legal dangers of industrialising procreation.

The Need for a Compassionate Response

The desire for children is one of the most powerful urges a human being will ever experience, second only perhaps to the self-preservation instinct (or alternatively, it may be said to form a part of the self-preservation instinct). In a world where infertility is becoming an evermore serious problem, the lure of technologies which offer miracle solutions is understandable. The suffering of infertile couples cannot be underestimated and is possibly even more acute in societies where being childless is vaunted as a positive and empowering choice.

Accounts by women of their experience of infertility and unfulfilled fertility make for distressing reading and serve as a constant reminder of the need to provide childless couples with pastoral support and understanding when prejudice and ignorance about infertility still abound. Nor should support be limited to the relatively brief period in couples' lives when they are actively trying for a baby. Infertility can haunt the human experience at every point in adult life: a woman will not be pregnant when her friends are pregnant, she will not be raising children when her friends have young children, she will not witness her children graduate, marry or have children of their own. A woman whose motherhood is thwarted will also have to struggle with the absence of grandchildren. There is no moment when the absence of much-desired children is easy to accept.

In her article "Accepting Childlessness after Infertility", writer Pamela Mahoney Tsigdinos describes an all-too-common sense of what she calls "disenfranchised grief" and the feeling that "most of the world didn't recognize our losses or offer any of the support reserved for legitimate grief",[37] a complaint also made by postabortive women and women who have experienced miscarriage.

In a frank reflection on living with involuntary childlessness, writer Mandy Appleyard expresses her own feelings of loss with painful eloquence:

> My life is a poorer place for not having children, and while I'm sure lots of women in my situation don't share my sentiments, I feel I am less of a woman—emotionally and physically—for not being a mother. There is a vast realm of experience and growth I will never know, and a love that will be forever unexpressed. I know that what any mother describes as the most profound love she has ever known is, to me, a locked door—that there is so much love I will never be able to give, wisdom and understanding I cannot share, shelter and solace I cannot provide.[38]

At a conference organised by the American Association of Fertility Care Practitioners in 2012, a fertility doctor specialising in NaPro Technology, Dr Phil Boyle, spoke of the need to take care of couples during treatment. He recognised the stress that can be involved in trying for a baby and the need to protect the couple's marriage from undue strain, to consider praying with them and also to ensure that the couple were prepared for the possibility that they

[37] Pamela Mahoney Tsigdinos, "Accepting Childlessness after Infertility", Seleni Institute, accessed 11 February 2017, http://seleni.org/advice-support /article/accepting-childlessness-after-infertility#sthash.nqZsGcfB.dpuf.

[38] Mandy Appleyard, " 'I'm Childless ... and That's Okay' ", *Red* online, April 2015, https://mandyappleyard.files.wordpress.com/2011/02/childless -memoir-in-red-magazine-april-2015.pdf.

would not have a baby. At the same conference, a platform was given to couples who had been helped to have a child through the pioneering work of Life Fertility, but at the end, a woman stood up and stated calmly that she had not been able to have a baby but she felt nevertheless that natural fertility appreciation had worked for her because she had accepted life without children.

The woman's intervention gave a voice to the untold thousands of women who are forced to accept a future without children and find ways to come to terms with the prospect. It was a timely reminder that when women are assisted by practitioners to make sense of their fertility, they may also be helped to make sense of infertility. A truly pro-woman approach to infertility does not exploit or endanger a woman's body or create and destroy human life at will, but nor does it abandon a woman to deal with childlessness alone.

The Lady Vanishes:
Abortion, Gendercide and the World's Missing Women

More girls have been killed in the last fifty years, precisely because they are girls, than men were killed in all the wars of the twentieth century combined. More girls are killed in this routine "gendercide" in any one decade than people were slaughtered in all the genocides of the twentieth century.

—Nicholas Kristof and Sheryl WuDunn, *Half the Sky*

What Is Gendercide?

The term "gendercide" was coined by Mary Anne Warren during the 1980s to describe deliberate acts of mass killing on grounds of gender, but the term has only recently started to appear in dictionaries. The term is usually used to refer to the killing of women, but "gendercide" is a neutral term which can apply to the deliberate killing of either men or women because of their sex (femicide and androcide refer more specifically to female and male killings).

In stating what gendercide is, it is also important to state what it is not. For example, male combatants in a theatre of war would not constitute victims of gendercide

Nicholas Kristof and Sheryl WuDunn, "Introduction", *Half the Sky* (London: Hatchette UK, 2010), https://www.thejc.com/news/israel/israeli-horror-as-sex-abuser-adopts-girl-4-1.45624.

as the targeting of armed men does not fit easily within the broader definition of genocide. By contrast, an occupying army who rounded up a civilian population, separated the men from the women and killed the men (the Kosovo massacre would be just one example) might constitute gendercide, in spite of the fact that the act is intended to reduce the potential pool of soldiers. The men in this scenario may be regarded by an enemy army as potential soldiers, but they are not combatants and are in no position to resist, rendering their deaths a clear act of mass murder.

It rarely escapes public attention when individuals— male or female—are put against a wall, but outside theatres of war, gendercide in the world today is less obvious yet occurs on a massive scale, and the victims of invisible gendercide are almost exclusively female.

The claim made in *Half the Sky* about the number of gendercide-related deaths outstripping the total number of war and genocide-related fatalities in the twentieth century may appear to be an outrageous claim when we consider that the twentieth century is widely accepted as having been the bloodiest in human history, but the raw data that has emerged in recent years highlighting the skewed sex ratios of countries such as India and China render it difficult to dismiss this allegation as rhetorical hyperbole. It is not before time that the issue of gendercide has become the subject of campaigning and heated debate, as it is one of the most pernicious social injustices against women of the current time.

Gendercide has always occurred in some form or other in virtually all cultures, mainly through infanticide and neglect, but with widespread access to abortion and technical advances such as cheap ultrasound scans, the elimination of baby girls is occurring earlier and earlier. For years, sex-selective abortion has been the elephant in the room in feminist circles with considerable levels of reluctance to discuss the subject at all, possibly out of fear that the abortion movement will be in some way undermined.

As early as 1997, UNICEF was making the claim that there were some sixty million "missing" girls in Asia due to gender violence[1] (equivalently the entire population of Britain), though during the same decade, economist and Nobel laureate Amartya Sen put the number at closer to one hundred million,[2] and the ActionAid report "Disappearing Daughters" (2009)[3] quoted a figure of thirty-five million missing girls in India alone, with the number of girls lost through sex-selective abortion continuing to increase.

The global figure for missing girls stands at an estimated 160 million.[4] A paper published in the *Lancet* in 2006 estimated that some ten million baby girls had been aborted in India over two decades,[5] with the Invisible Girl Project claiming that more baby girls are aborted in India and China every year than the total number of girls born in the United States, amounting to a baby girl aborted in India at a rate of one a minute.[6]

[1] "60 Million Women 'Missing' because of Gender Discrimination", UNICEF, Information Newsline, accessed 11 February 2017, http://www.unicef.org/newsline/97pr28a.htm.

[2] Sunny Hundal, "India's 60 Million Women That Never Were", Aljazeera.com, 8 August 2013, http://www.aljazeera.com/indepth/opinion/2013/07/201372814110570679.html.

[3] Annie Kelly, "Disappearing Daughters", ActionAid, accessed 11 February 2017, http://www.actionaid.org.uk/sites/default/files/doc_lib/disappearing_daughters_0608.pdf.

[4] Jimmy Carter, "Patriarchy and Violence against Women and Girls", *Lancet*, 20 November 2014, http://www.thelancet.com/journals/lancet/article/PIIS0140-6736(14)62217-0/fulltext.

[5] Steve Connor, "The Lost Girls: It Seems That the Global War on Girls Has Arrived in Britain", *Independent*, 14 January 2014, http://www.independent.co.uk/news/science/the-lost-girls-it-seems-that-the-global-war-on-girls-has-arrived-in-britain-9059610.html.

[6] "The Issue", Invisible Girl Project, accessed 11 February 2017, http://invisiblegirlproject.org/see-the-issue/.

Contrary to popular belief, gender imbalance is not an exclusively rural problem, fuelled by traditional practices or the need to produce boys to work on farms. There is evidence to suggest that sex-selective abortion is even more of a problem among affluent city dwellers who want the social cache of a son and have the means to pay for what they want.[7]

A healthy sex ratio should be more or less 1:1, though it is common for there to be some natural fluctuations in sex ratios, usually around 105:100 (male/female) to allow for the fact that boys are more likely than girls to die of natural causes and accidents.[8] India's sex ratio is skewed across the population, but according to the 2011 Census, the gender imbalance in the zero-to-six age group is at its worst since independence.[9]

During heated debates, I have been presented with the serious argument that a shortage of women should increase their value within society. On the face of it, this is a perfectly logical argument, or it would be if women were products such as cars or foodstuffs to be bought and sold in the marketplace. It would also make sense if the destruction of human life had no impact upon the perpetrators or survivors themselves, and it is here that the analogy falls down. The violent killing of unborn baby girls is hardly

[7] Raywat Deonandan, "Implications of India's Skewed Sex Ratio", *Internet Journal of Public Health* 2, no. 1 (2012): 2, https://www.ruor.uottawa.ca /bitstream/10393/22752/3/Deonandan_Raywat_2012_Implications_of _Indias_skewed_sex_ratio.pdf.

[8] World Health Organization, South-East Asia Region, "Sex Ratio, Population Sex Ratio", accessed 4 January 2018, http://www.searo.who.int/entity /health_situation_trends/data/chi/sex-ratio/en/.

[9] Siwan Anderson and Debraj Ray, "The Age Distribution of Missing Women in India", *Economic & Political Weekly* 47, nos. 47 and 48 (1 December 2012): 87, http://www.econ.nyu.edu/user/debraj/Papers/AndersonRayIndia .pdf.

akin to the deliberate burning of a field of wheat to increase the market value. The crossing of such a primordial moral barrier can only have a negative impact upon society.

The consequences of skewed sex ratios for women are consistently negative and far-reaching, including an increase in instances of rape, wife-sharing, baby smuggling and sex trafficking. Dr B. S. Dahiya, a former senior government official, gave this stark warning over a decade ago: "Violence against women is rising. We'll have more unnatural practices, such as brothers sharing a wife. In a few years, no woman will be safe. There will be abductions and rapes, even of minors."[10]

This warning was echoed more recently by the Council of Europe, commenting on the increasingly skewed sex ratio in countries such as Albania, Armenia, Azerbaijan and Georgia. According to the Council of Europe, sex-selective abortion is "likely to create difficulties for men to find spouses, lead to serious human rights violations such as forced prostitution, trafficking for the purpose of marriage or sexual exploitation, and contribute to a rise in criminality and social unrest".[11]

In China, the expression "bare branches" is used to describe young men who cannot find a wife and establish a family. There are now some forty million men in China—the majority in rural areas—who will never be able to marry and establish families of their own. Within China, some of the consequences emerging from the nation's skewed set ratios include the reemergence of undesirable marriage practices, including child brides, marriage

[10] Reported in the *Times* of London, 22 June 2004.
[11] Doris Stump, "Pre-Natal Sex Selection", Parliamentary Assembly, Committee on Equal Opportunities for Women and Men, accessed 11 February 2017, http://www.assembly.coe.int/CommitteeDocs/2011/ASEGAselection prenatalee.pdf.

purchase and levirate marriages, where a widow is obliged to marry her dead husband's brother. Other consequences blamed on gendercide are the steep increase in promiscuity, trafficking, use of prostitutes and the spread of sexually transmitted diseases, particularly in areas with high numbers of bare branches.[12]

Amartya Sen made his prophetic warnings about the world's millions of "missing women" twenty-five years ago and warned unequivocally that gender-based abortions constituted a new form of sex discrimination. He wrote: "Selective abortion of female foetuses—what can be called 'natality discrimination'—is a kind of high-tech manifestation of preference for boys."[13]

It has taken a generation for those warnings to be taken seriously, and millions of lives have been lost during those squandered years.

Causes

It is straightforward enough to discuss what gendercide is and how it is carried out, but the first and largest question is surely *why*? What is it that causes parents, extended families and the broader society to reject the fundamental value of women so comprehensively as to deny girls the right to be born? It is a huge question and one for which there

---

[12] Quanbao Jiang and Jesús J. Sánchez-Barricarte, "The Predicament of Bare Branches' Sexuality", *Electronic Journal of Human Sexuality* 15 (18 September 2012), http://www.ejhs.org/volume15/Bare.html.

[13] Keith Perry, "Illegal Abortion of Female Foetuses by Some Ethnic Groups Who Favour Sons Has Reduced Female Population", *Telegraph*, 15 January 2014, http://www.telegraph.co.uk/news/religion/10572870/Illegal-abortion-of-female-foetuses-by-some-ethnic-groups-who-favour-sons-has-reduced-female-population.html.

are no easy or straightforward answers as the reasons for
son preference are deeply embedded in cultures and belief
systems around the world.

Gendercide represents the bloody conclusion to an
ingrained misogyny that has always seen women as a
liability—the weaker sex, the lesser man—and women's
struggles for full emancipation have been the subject of
thousands of books, doctoral theses and political tracts over
the past two hundred years as different societies have grap-
pled with the reasons for discrimination against women.
Gendercide takes an ancient belief that girls' lives are
inherently expendable to its brutal extreme.

"Cultural context" can never justify genocidal behaviour, but it is important to be aware of the specific
cultural and economic considerations which contribute
to son preference in some countries. Much is said about
India's dowry system, which can make having a daughter cripplingly expensive for a family. The dowry system was prohibited in 1961, but it continues unabated,
and dowry-related deaths, including bride-burning, have
risen since the passing of that Act, with India's National
Crime Research Bureau reporting that there were 7,634
dowry-related deaths of women in 2015, the equivalent of
twenty-one lives a day.[14]

A related factor is that of the patrilocal tradition, a common practice within societies where gendercide occurs.
This is the tradition of women going to live with the husband's parents rather than the groom joining her family,
resulting in the woman caring for her husband's parents in

---

[14] Chayyanika Nigam, "21 Lives Lost to Dowry Every Day Across India;
Conviction Rate Less Than 35 Per Cent", *India Today*, 22 April 2017, http://
indiatoday.intoday.in/story/dowry-deaths-national-crime-records-bureau
-conviction-rate/1/935341.html.

old age rather than her own. In societies without a welfare state, the elderly are entirely dependent upon their children to support them, and the prospect of a daughter growing up to leave the parental home to support others may present an elderly couple with serious difficulties—hence the saying "Daughters are raised to water other people's gardens."[15]

Other issues—financial and practical but also religious—may play their part in the perpetuation of gendercide: inheritance exclusively through the male line; the need in rural communities for boys to help out on farms; religious sensibilities such as the significance of a son lighting his father's funeral pyre; the belief, however little admitted, that a boy is a blessing and a girl a curse.

For this reason, the tendency to create small disparities in sex ratios has always existed, but with the arrival of ultrasound and much more widely practised abortion, the problem has escalated and abortion has become a major factor in the mounting demographic crisis. However, whereas some groups are beginning to speak openly about the dangers of sex-selective abortion, there still tends to be an awkwardness and evasiveness about talking about abortion itself, and instead a great deal is said in very general terms about the need to change cultural prejudices.

Sex-Selective Abortion's Apologists

What might be termed "abortion loyalism" diverts attention away from any honest discussion of the part abortion

---

[15] Gesu Antonio Báez, "Raising a Daughter Is Like Watering Your Neighbor's Garden: The Fatal Mentality from the Indian Subcontinent and Female Infanticide", Blog, 19 January 2014, http://www.jesusanthonybaez.com/blog /raising-a-daughter-is-like-watering-your-neighbors-garden.

plays in the elimination of girls, but in its most dogmatic form, abortion loyalism insists upon defending abortion at all costs, under all circumstances, even if it means defending the elimination of baby girls or tacitly supporting the bullying of women into sex-selective abortions by patriarchal forces.

A particularly crass example of this abortion loyalism came in the form of the following argument by a journalist in a respected British broadsheet newspaper: "What about when a pregnant woman lives in a society that gives her real and considerable reason to fear having a girl? The kind of society where dowry systems mean an inconveniently gendered child could bankrupt a family, or one where a livid patriarch deprived of a male heir could turn his fury on both mother and daughter? In those situations, a woman wouldn't just be justified in seeking sex selective abortion; she'd be thoroughly rational to do so."[16]

It seems a little incongruous to read a self-proclaimed feminist arguing in favour of sacrificing the lives of baby girls in the name of appeasing violent misogyny and thereby perpetuating it indefinitely. Moreover, it is debatable as to whether women in countries where gendercide is rife feel quite so philosophical about the antenatal discrimination faced by millions of females or appreciate the moral equivocation of Western feminists desperate to protect their own ideological interests. Cultural context provides motivations not excuses, and there is a shameless hypocrisy associated with groups who attempt to impose Western gender ideology on developing countries without making any concessions whatsoever to cultural

---

[16] Sarah Ditum, "Why Women Have a Right to Sex-Selective Abortion", *Guardian*, 19 September 2013, http://www.theguardian.com/commentisfree/2013/sep/19/sex-selective-abortion-womans-right.

sensitivities, only to play the "cultural sensitivity" card when abortion is being used as a weapon against women. As one campaigner for an antigendercide group warned: "In 20 years, one fifth of the women in India will have been systematically exterminated. This is the genocidal targeting of a group by a society in whichever way it can. So it's odd to talk about 'changing mindsets' as the method of stopping this mass extermination of women, when we wouldn't do that for the mass extermination of any other group."[17]

By way of analogy, if a minority group were being massacred by a regime upholding racist principles, it is unlikely that any aid agency or campaigning organisation claiming to stand for human rights would merely promote the need to understand the cultural context and perhaps to fund outreach and educational programmes, so as to change the climate in which genocidal attacks occur.

As a result of an unsuccessful attempt by a British politician to introduce legislation to ban sex-selective abortion, evidence emerged from groups which backed Fiona Bruce's campaign, which backed up the claim made by opponents of sex-selective abortion that women in Britain are bullied and threatened with violence and divorce if they refuse to abort an unwanted baby girl. The director of the women's organisation Jeena International, Rani Bilkhu, spoke to the press about the charity's work with women who have suffered abuse as a result of being pregnant with a baby girl and made the observation: "Women are aborting for many diverse reasons, from ensuring equity in their family and community, domestic violence,

[17] Vanessa Baird, "Sex, Lies and Complicity in India", 8 January 2014, *New Internationalist*, http://newint.org/features/web-exclusive/2014/01/08/sex -selection-feminism-india/#sthash.7hDrg8yo.dpuf.

and being culturally enslaved to believe that their status, marriage, value will be elevated."[18]

No humanitarian organisation which claims to uphold the rights of women can argue that supporting a practice that is in itself discriminatory marks a positive step for women. The emphasis should be on stopping the practice and protecting women at risk of abuse. As Sajda Mughal of JAN Trust warned at the time of the parliamentary debate: "Our experience tells us that practical help is needed in communities where women are sometimes devalued and degraded to the extent that people try to stop a female from being born."[19]

However, the argument that performing a sex-selective abortion on an unwilling woman is somehow humane because it prevents her from being beaten into a miscarriage was used seriously by some lobby groups to campaign against a ban on sex-selective abortion. As journalist Tim Stanley pointed out when the debate was at its most intense: "This argument implies that the state ought to ignore or even assist those men who pressure their partners to have abortions. It would make far more sense for society to oppose sex selective abortion and the chauvinism that makes it happen, rather than lamely accepting that some men will always hate women."[20]

A serious obstacle to discussing gendercide in Britain (and this may well be similar in other developed countries)

[18] Imran Choudhury, "Action Sought on Forced Abortions", *Eastern Eye*, 20 February 2015, https://www.easterneye.eu/news/detail/action-sought-on-forced-abortions.

[19] Ibid.

[20] Tim Stanley, "The Left Is Fanatical about Abortion; Here, at Last, Is the Proof", *Telegraph*, 27 February 2015, http://www.telegraph.co.uk/women/womens-politics/11439592/The-Left-is-fanatical-about-abortion.-Here-at-last-is-the-proof.html.

is the persistent denial of its existence among abortion promoters. Some years before gendercide began to be openly discussed in Britain, two journalists were involved in an undercover investigation in which they filmed doctors who were prepared to arrange abortions because the couple said that they didn't want a baby girl, including one doctor who glibly admitted that it was a form of "female infanticide".[21] The undercover film made waves at the time, with many, including those who would normally be in favour of abortion, genuinely disgusted by footage of doctors smilingly agreeing to dispose of an unwanted baby girl.

During a parliamentary debate on the subject, MPs who support abortion were quick to express their objections to sex-selective abortions. Emily Thornberry, an ardently pro-abortion politician, stated:

> Gender-based abortion is part of a complex of misogynistic beliefs and practices to which we cannot give an inch. Along with female infanticide, it is the purest expression of the belief that the male is more valuable than the female, for invariably gender-based abortion involves the destruction of female fetuses; we do not hear of male fetuses being aborted.
>
> Women are not the weaker sex. We are not a curse. We are not a burden to be disposed of as a family sees fit. What is more, people have to be completely myopic not to see that if it becomes known that doctors are taking a no-questions-asked attitude to gender-selective abortions, women will be pressurised into having them.

[21] "Abortion Investigation: Doctor Filmed Admitting Termination Would Be 'Infanticide'", *The Telegraph*, 23 February 2012, http://www.telegraph .co.uk/news/health/news/9102160/Abortion-investigation-doctor-filmed -admitting-termination-would-be-infanticide.html.

Gender-selective abortions are at root an exercise of patriarchal and communal coercion, not female choice.[22]

Tellingly, the reaction from the biggest proponents
of abortion was to support sex-selective abortion as just
another choice, or to deny that it happens at all. An article
putting the case for sex-selective abortion claimed that staff
at BPAS (British Pregnancy Advisory Service) facilities say
that "the only time a woman walks in and requests an
abortion because the fetus is the 'wrong gender' is when
she's a journalist".[23] This claim was thrown into doubt by
a former medical director of the very same organisation,
Dr Vincent Argent, who had previously stated that covert
sex-selective abortion was widespread and occurred in all
communities.[24] This was corroborated by an investigation
conducted by the *Independent*, which uncovered clear evidence that sex-selective abortion does occur in some parts
of Britain.[25] The government attempted to whitewash
the issue, claiming that its own investigations had found
no evidence of sex-selective abortion in Britain, but the

[22] House of Commons Archive, 9 October 2013, Column 103WH, https://
publications.parliament.uk/pa/cm201314/cmhansrd/cm131009/halltext
/131009h0002.htm.

[23] Ann Furedi, "You Can't Be Pro-Choice Only When You Like the
Choice", Spiked Online, 16 September 2013, http://www.spiked-online.com
/newsite/article/you_cant_be_pro_choice_only_when_you_like_the_choice
/14032#.Wk4tQGhl_IU.

[24] Claire Newell and Holly Watt, "Sex-Selection Abortions are 'Widespread'", *Telegraph*, 24 February 2012, http://www.telegraph.co.uk/health
/healthnews/9104994/Sex-selection-abortions-are-widespread.html.

[25] Steve Connor, "The Lost Girls: Illegal Abortion Widely Used by Some
UK Ethnic Groups to Avoid Daughters 'Has Reduced Female Population
by between 1,500 and 4,700'", *Independent*, 2014, http://www.independent
.co.uk/news/science/the-lost-girls-illegal-abortion-widely-used-by-some-uk
-ethnic-groups-to-avoid-daughters-has-reduced-female-population-by-between
-1500-and-4700-9059790.html.

Independent found that around one in ten girls were missing among certain ethnic groups in this country.

What the newspaper did which led them to the conclusion—independently verified by statisticians—that sex-selective abortion does occur in Britain was to look at the sex of second children onwards. This is very significant because if there is a son preference, a couple are much more likely to welcome a baby girl if she comes first. A couple might console themselves that they might have a son next time. Where the figures become suspicious is when a disproportionately large number of second children are boys where the first is a girl. This was what the *Independent* investigators found when they analysed the statistics, and the sex ratio became progressively more skewed the further down the line the child came in the family.

The same was found to be true in both Canadian and American studies. In some cases, the disparity is very significant. According to the UN Population Fund, in Armenia, the sex ratio for a first and second child is more or less normal; the sex ratio for a third child is 175:100 girls.[26] An even bigger gender disparity was found in China in cases where a second child is permitted, along with a larger average age gap between children where the first is a girl and the second a boy, suggesting but not conclusively proving that there was an abortion between those births.

Gendercide and Maternal Health

A more complex but no less deadly facet of gendercide can be found when the preference for a boy over a girl

[26] United Nations Population Fund, *Report of the International Workshop on Skewed Sex Ratios at Birth: Addressing the Issue and the Way Forward*, Ha Noi, Viet Nam, 5–6 October 2011, p. 10, http://www.unfpa.org/sites/default/files/resource-pdf/Report_SexRatios_2012.pdf.

manifests itself more subtly, influencing the care the mother receives during pregnancy. However, this influence can be extremely difficult for members of the medical profession to prove. Some maternal health charities such as Matercare International, a Canada-based group of Catholic obstetricians and gynaecologists, speak of domestic violence happening both by commission and by omission—that is, by an act of violence or through a deliberate failure to act—for example, refusing to give a woman the maternity care she requires to deliver her baby safely where there is an obvious duty of care. This is a controversial position because there is considerable debate surrounding the extent to which a person can be said to have a moral duty to help another, and some might argue that neglect is morally wrong where there is a duty to act, but it may not be the same as violence unless the harm caused by the omission was actually intended.

By way of an example, let us consider for a moment the following scenarios, inspired by the real-life experiences of an Indian obstetrician.[27] A woman in labour is brought in, and the family insist for no clinical reason that she must have a caesarean. This raises immediate suspicions among the doctors as caesarean section is a very expensive operation, but the procedure goes ahead and the obstetrician is not surprised when he delivers a baby boy. On another occasion, he encounters the reverse scenario: a woman is brought in, but the family does everything possible to obstruct the doctors, including refusing permission for a caesarean. The woman will eventually deliver a dead or dying baby girl. In both cases, the doctor is fairly certain that the family knew all along whether the mother

[27]Jeevan Kuruvilla, "The Boy Longed for ... and the Unwanted Girl(s)", *The Learner* (blog), 31 January 2012, http://jeevankuruvilla.blogspot.in/2012 /01boy-longed-for-and-unwanted-girls.html.

was carrying a girl or a boy and made decisions about the delivery based on that knowledge, but such a suspicion is almost impossible to prove unless the family themselves admit it. How can he seek justice for that woman and her child without evidence, even if his every instinct tells him that gender discrimination has been at work?

China and Gendercide

There is an old Chinese proverb that it is better to have one crippled son than eight healthy daughters. It is therefore no surprise that China currently has one of the worst gender imbalances in the world. The cultural son preference has been exacerbated by the country's brutal birth-control policy, which has been and continues to be responsible for many terrible atrocities against women. In terms of fuelling China's skewed sex ratios, it continues to have a catastrophic impact with ratios at their worst in the youngest age groups.[28] According to the US Congressional Executive Commission on China, the average male-to-female sex ratio in the infant-to-four-year-old age group in China is 123.26:100, with two provinces recording ratios of over 140:100 in that age group.[29] Interestingly, the only two provinces shown to have sex ratios within normal boundaries—Tibet and Xinjiang—are largely inhabited by minority groups with more lenient birth-control laws.

---

[28] "'Gendercide' Is the Systematic Killing of Members of a Specific Gender, Either Males or Females", Women's Rights without Frontiers, accessed 29 December 2017, http://www.womensrightswithoutfrontiers.org/index.php ?nav=gendercide.

[29] Congressional-Executive Commission on China, "Population Planning Demographic Consequences", 2010 Annual Report, January 2010, https:// www.cecc.gov/publications/annual-reports/2010-annual-report#popplan demography.

China's birth-control policy may well have been responsible for female deaths by infanticide as well as through sex-selective abortion. In his book *A Mother's Ordeal*, Steve Mosher retells the story of a family in rural China who murdered their five-year-old daughter when the mother became pregnant with an illegal second child.[30] They knew it would be impossible to obtain a second birth permit and resented the daughter for obstructing the birth of a possible son. The crime was quickly uncovered after villagers became suspicious, and the girl's father and his pregnant wife were executed.

Shocking though the story is, infanticide is not a negligible risk for girls who are fortunate enough to survive gestation but who are born into countries and cultures where gendercide is practised. In India, infant mortality is 75 percent higher among girls compared with boys because of infanticide but also because of the abuse and neglect of girls. Some 20 percent of India's missing girls in the under-twenty age group were born; the majority may perish before birth, but around 20 percent are lost sometime during childhood or adolescence.[31]

Grieving Mothers

The effects on the mothers themselves should not be forgotten. Gendercide makes victims of women at every level, from the unborn baby girls who die, to the infant girls who are neglected to death, to the grown women and girls who suffer the indirect consequences of gendercide.

---

[30] Steve Mosher, *A Mother's Ordeal: One Woman's Fight against China's One-Child Policy* (New York: Harcourt Brace Jovanovich, 1993).

[31] United Nations Population Fund, *Report of the International Workshop on Skewed Sex Ratios*, p. 10.

But the women pressured into having sex-selective abortions experience total loss of bodily integrity, loss of their daughters and lost motherhood.

In the course of my research, I have read passionate assurances by the senior staff of abortion facilities that women in Britain are not left in the position where they are forced to undergo an abortion they do not want, that they are identified and empowered to make the choice they really want to make, without any indication being given as to how this happens in practice.[32] The fantasy world of every abortion a wanted abortion is very wide of the mark at the best of times, but when it comes to sex-selective abortion it is particularly far from the reality. Women like Samira (not her real name) give the lie to the notion that abortion facilities show any great skill or even willingness to identify these at-risk women. Samira agreed to speak to journalists about her ordeal at a time when Britain's political elite were still in denial about the reality of sex-selective abortion. She said:

> On the day of the termination I went into the clinic crying. I was crying and crying and could not stop.... The nurse saw I was upset but she said "just put these tablets inside you". They weren't concerned that this person looked upset. I was crying but I was trying to be careful because what if they didn't go ahead with the abortion and then my husband would blame me.
>
> I just wanted them to stop. I just wanted to run away from there, but the thing was, where would I run away to? What would I do? The last day before I had the abortion I said to him [husband] very clearly that what he was doing

---

[32] Shaheen Hashmat, "Sex Selective Abortion and Honour Based Violence", Blog, 12 February 2015, http://www.shaheenhashmat.com/sex -selective-abortion-and-honour-based-violence/#.VTYMayHBzGc.

was wrong.... I felt I couldn't make the choice on my own because if I'd made that choice and gone ahead with the baby then he would actually end the pregnancy himself. He would probably beat me up to such a state that there would probably be no pregnancy inside me. I was scared of that.

The worse thing was, when I went in, I had a bump, and when I came out there was no bump. I kept touching it and I just wanted to scream but the noise wouldn't come out.... I wanted my baby back.[33]

At an international workshop on skewed sex ratios in 2011, it was noted with concern that there tends to be far more information available about the effects of gender imbalance on men than on women—for example, the bare branches phenomenon in China, the plight of men unable to marry and so forth—and campaigners against gendercide must beware of unwittingly relegating women to the role of caretakers or instruments in the improvement of the health of society. It is not in the interests of any section of society for women to be eliminated from the population before birth, and gendercide will continue to have serious implications for societies around the world until it is properly addressed by politicians, by the medical profession and by feminists themselves. We owe it to society and especially to women, those born and unborn, to put an end to this injustice.

[33] Steve Connor, " 'I Had to Terminate My Pregnancies Because I Was Carrying Girls'—The Story of a Woman Forced into Gender-Selective Abortions", *The Independent*, 17 March 2014.

Dancing on Women's Graves:
Maternal Mortality and the
International Abortion Lobby

Women are not dying because of a disease we cannot treat. They are dying because societies have yet to make the decision that their lives are worth saving.

— Mahmoud Fathalla, president of the International
Federation of Gynaecology and Obstetrics

On 20 April 2006, I lay in a hospital bed in my local maternity hospital. It had been a rough day by all accounts. I had woken up in the early hours of the morning to feel my waters breaking; the sudden, unexpected experience of extreme pain, far too severe to be normal in early labour, caused me to make the journey to the hospital. Without examining me, a midwife gave me a smile, bullied me into signing a document claiming that I felt well and wanted to leave the hospital and I was discharged, screaming in agony all the way to the waiting taxi. As a young, first-time mum overwhelmed with exhaustion and panic, I failed to appreciate the seriousness of the situation I was in, believing that

Mahmoud Fathalla, *On Safe Motherhood at 25 Years: Looking Back, Moving Forwards* (Dorchester, UK: Hands on for Mothers and Babies), p. 10, accessed 9 January 2018, https://www.birmingham.ac.uk/Documents/heroes/on-safe-motherhood-fathalla.pdf.

I was going through a normal labour, and when a midwife reassured me over the phone that my sudden blood loss was "just a show", I chose to believe her. It was over an hour before I arrived back at the hospital, still bleeding steadily, having been told there was no need to rush.

That had been the morning. Now, it was approaching midnight, and I hardly knew where I was any longer. I had some sense that I was dying and my baby was dying; I drifted in and out of consciousness, shocked into wakefulness every couple of minutes by the feeling that someone was swinging a baseball bat against the base of my spine, but it was becoming harder to scream. My mouth and throat were dry, and the blood loss had left me weak and listless.

Suddenly, an obstetrician was at my side with a look of restrained panic on his face. I did not know it then because there was no time for him to explain, but besides the heavy bleeding, he had discovered other complications. The reason for the hours of excruciating pain and exhaustion were simple—my labour was obstructed. I heard the doctor issuing orders to a team of nurses and other medics, then felt myself being rushed in the direction of the operating theatre. Minutes later, I had been given a spinal anaesthesia and a highly skilled obstetrics team had cut my baby out of my body alive. As I passed out, I heard the sound of my son giving a shrill, unforgettable birth cry.

It haunted me afterwards that if I had not had access to a well-equipped hospital, trained obstetricians, an operating theatre and the drugs necessary to prevent me from bleeding to death, my twenty-four-year-old husband would have lost everything that night and been left to face the future alone. And I am haunted still by the thought that I have during four births been spared a death sentence from which thousands of women and babies in developing countries face no reprieve.

Facts and Figures

As with any attempt at gathering global statistics, accurate numbers are very difficult to calculate for a number of reasons. The first is poor reporting in some countries, or indeed, no reporting of maternal death at all. There can also be significant differences in methods of reporting and definitions of maternal death, meaning that estimates vary from between 350,000 and 600,000 maternal deaths a year, 99 percent of which occur in developing countries.

According to the CIA World Factbook,[1] the countries with the highest maternal mortality rate (MMR)[2] are the following:

1. Sierra Leone   1,360 deaths per 100,000 live births (2015 EST.)
2. Central African Republic   862 deaths per 100,000 live births (2015 EST.)
3. Chad   856 deaths per 100,000 live births (2015 EST.)

By comparison, the MMR for the United States, the United Kingdom and Ireland are the following:

United States   14 deaths per 100,000 births (2015 EST.)

United Kingdom   9 deaths per 100,000 births (2015 EST.)

Ireland   8 deaths per 100,000 births (2015 EST.)

[1] Central Intelligence Agency, World Factbook, accessed 12 February 2017, https://www.cia.gov/library/publications/resources/the-world-factbook/rankorder/2223rank.html.

[2] MMR is defined as the annual number of female deaths per 100,000 live births from any cause related to pregnancy and childbirth.

The discrepancy between maternal deaths in developing and developed countries is clearly massive, though it is also worth noting that there is a discrepancy within developed countries themselves, with traditionally pro-life countries such as Ireland, Poland and Malta being labelled backward and indifferent to women's lives in spite of having significantly lower death rates than countries with permissive abortion laws.

The good news is that global maternal mortality rates are in decline and have decreased by around 43 percent over a period of twenty-five years, according to the WHO.[3] However, the decline remains slow, the Millennium Development Goal of reducing maternal mortality by 75 percent were not met and women continue to die unnecessarily.

Causes

The two biggest causes of maternal death are haemorrhage and sepsis. Haemorrhage is the single biggest cause of maternal death anywhere in the world, accounting for around one quarter of all cases and a third of cases in sub-Saharan Africa, followed by sepsis, which accounts for approximately 10 percent of deaths. A less common but particularly horrific cause of death is obstructed labour, where the baby becomes stuck in the birth canal and the mother may be maimed for life or die having spent days in terrible pain trying to deliver a baby who may also die in the process. This is particularly common among very

[3] World Health Organization, Global Health Observatory (GHO) Data, "Maternal Mortality", accessed 12 February 2017, http://www.who.int/gho /maternal_health/mortality/maternal_mortality_text/en/.

young or malnourished mothers whose pelvises are too small for them to deliver naturally. Other causes, direct and indirect, include preeclampsia, heart disease, malaria and anaemia, but there are many.

What is particularly dangerous about haemorrhage is that there is very little time to treat it. If a woman starts bleeding during labour, she may have up to twelve hours; if she has a postpartum bleed, she has less than two hours before bleeding to death. Therefore, if a woman is giving birth in a remote area, miles away from the nearest hospital, without easy access to affordable or suitable transport, she is highly unlikely to receive help in time. If a hospital is within easy reach but there is no blood bank and relatives have to be rounded up as donors, time may run out for the woman. Some years ago, in an article for the British newspaper *Pro-Life Times*, I described a teenage girl in sub-Saharan Africa who had gone into labour with twins.[4] She managed to deliver them both in a hospital, though with minimal medical assistance, only to begin bleeding heavily postpartum. There was only one doctor available, and it took an hour and a half for her to receive treatment, by which time it was too late and she died shortly afterwards. In this case, there was an accessible hospital, the technology was available but the hospital was so short-staffed that help could not be provided in time.

Beyond the clinical causes of death, there are many other reasons why women die in childbirth, all of which need to be considered. These include the more obvious causes: lack of accessible antenatal care where certain health problems could be picked up in good time; lack of good obstetric care and facilities such as equipped operating theatres

[4] Fiorella Nash, "The Worldwide Scandal Which Demands a Pro-life Response", *Pro-Life Times* 49, May 2011.

and cheap antibiotics; the shortage of trained birth attendants; but also broader issues such as poor infrastructure,
for example.

A paper published in the *Journal of Sustainable Development in Africa* in 2010 found that "despite the recognition
of the role of transport to development and the liveli-
hoods of poor people, rural transport networks, in most
developing countries, are underdeveloped and of poor
quality (Lebo & Schelling, 2001). It is estimated that about
900 million rural dwellers in developing countries do not
have reliable, all season access to main road networks and
about 300 million do not have motorized access at all
(Lebo & Schelling, 2001)."[5]

A particularly heartbreaking example of this was highlighted in an Al Jazeera report[6] on maternal mortality
in Malawi, which until recently had one of the highest
maternal death rates in the world. A midwife in a remote
village was interviewed about her work, and she described
a young woman suffering a postpartum haemorrhage. The
only transport the family could find to get her to the nearest hospital was a wheelbarrow. The midwife watched
the barrow filling with blood, and the girl died before she
reached the hospital.

The most significant cause of all, however, is the poor
status of women in many parts of the world, which renders
it difficult for women to access medical care in time even
if it is readily available. As mentioned at the beginning of

[5] Michael Poku-Boansi, Ellis Ekekpe and Agatha Akua Bonney, "Com-
bating Maternal Mortality in the Gushegu District of Ghana: The Role of
Rural Transportation", *Journal of Sustainable Development in Africa* 12, no. 5
(2010): 274–75, http://www.jsd-africa.com/Jsda/V12No5_Fall2010_A/PDF
/Combating%20Maternal%20Mortality%20in%20the%20Gushegu%20
District%20of%20Ghana%20(Poku-Boansi,%20Ekekpe,%20Bonney).pdf.

[6] Al Jazeera, "Maternal Mortality", *Everywoman*, 18 January 2008.

this chapter, Mahmoud Fathalla, president of the International Federation of Gynaecology and Obstetrics, commented: "Women are not dying because of a disease we cannot treat. They are dying because societies have yet to make the decision that their lives are worth saving."

This belief was echoed by obstetricians interviewed in a documentary film produced with the assistance of the Pakistan Medical Association, charting developments in maternal health provision in Pakistan.[7] Obstetricians cited their own experience of families refusing to bring mothers to hospitals when they lived "hardly a kilometre away" until the women were already in serious danger of death or to refuse to pay for lifesaving treatment for the woman. This sense of frustration that women simply do not matter enough is repeated in virtually any discussion on maternal mortality. If the tragedy of maternal mortality is to be taken seriously, women must first be taken seriously, not regarded as expendable or predestined to die prematurely.

Infant Mortality

It is impossible to convey the full horror of young women dying unattended in terrible fear and agony, leaving behind devastated families and other children whose own survival may well be jeopardised by the loss of a mother. It is necessary to remember that millions of children die in infancy every year in developing countries and that there are strong direct and indirect connections between maternal and infant death.

---

[7] Steve Watson, *Working to Reduce Maternal Mortality in Pakistan* (E&B Media, 2009), https://www.youtube.com/watch?v=YqizJwxh_AQ&t=20s.

Infant mortality is the death of a child under the age of one and, like maternal death, it is taken as an indicator of the state of a nation's health.

In the United States, the infant mortality rate is 5.80 per 1,000 live births (2016); in Britain, the rate is 4.30 per 1,000 live births (2016), compared with Afghanistan, which currently has the highest infant mortality rate in the world, where the rate is *112.80* per 1,000 live births (2016).[8]

The picture is, if anything, more desperate when it comes to the deaths of under-fives. Around 5.9 million under-fives die every year from largely preventable causes, amounting to around 16,000 a day. As with maternal mortality, the infant mortality rate is decreasing, but the number of preventable infant deaths is still unacceptably high in developing countries.[9] A significant proportion of those deaths—some 45 percent, according to the WHO—are neo-natal: that is, a death occurring up to twenty-eight days after birth.[10] Maternal death is a key factor. According to USAID (US Agency for International Development),

The impact can be staggering—research published in 2003 showed that infants in Nepal whose mothers died during childbirth were 52 times more likely to die between the fourth and 24th week of life than children whose mothers survived childbirth. Surviving children

[8] Central Intelligence Agency, World Factbook, "Country Comparison: Infant Mortality Rate", accessed 12 February 2017, https://www.cia.gov /library/publications/resources/the-world-factbook/rankorder/2091rank.html.

[9] World Health Organization, Global Health Observatory (GHO) Data, "Under-Five Mortality", accessed 12 February 2017, http://www.who.int /gho/child_health/mortality/mortality_under_five_text/en/.

[10] World Health Organization, Global Health Observatory (GHO) Data, "Neonatal Mortality", accessed 12 February 2017, http://www.who.int/gho /child_health/mortality/neonatal_text/en/.

face consequences of family impoverishment (diminished resources for the children in particular), malnutrition, and decreased educational opportunities as older children leave school to earn money or care for their homes and younger siblings.[11]

In cultures around the world, the mother is the invisible, irreplaceable lynchpin of the family, and if she goes, the entire family is shattered.

The Lessons of History

There is always a great danger of complacency in the West when we think about maternal health. Very few people growing up in the United States or Europe will ever, mercifully, know a woman who dies in childbirth, and maternal mortality can feel rather like the stuff of Victorian melodrama. However, it is not so long ago in our own history that everyone would have known a woman who had died in childbirth. Maternal mortality in Britain went from being a major public health concern to a rare event in a remarkably short space of time.

Any discussion of the causes and solutions to maternal mortality around the world should surely begin with the questions, *why* and *how* has maternal mortality been successfully tackled in some countries and not in others? Furthermore, what lessons can we learn from countries where maternal mortality has been, for the most part, consigned to history?

---

[11] US Agency for International Development, "Two Decades of Progress: USAID's Child Survival and Maternal Health Program", accessed 12 February 2017, http://pdf.usaid.gov/pdf_docs/PDACN044.pdf.

A paper published in the *American Journal of Clinical Nutrition*[12] found that maternal mortality remained very high in Britain—apart from some peaks and troughs—between 1850, when records began to be meticulously kept, and the mid-1930s. It then began declining so definitely and so sustainably that maternal mortality went from being a serious public health problem to a notable public health success story within the space of fifteen to twenty years. This decline continued, albeit more gradually, into the 1960s, a pattern that was repeated in other northern European countries and the United States.

The decline was so dramatic that the authors of the paper note that there is now no cause of death for which there is a greater disparity between the developed and the developing world than the disparity in maternal mortality rates.

Irvine Loudon's paper reveals some interesting facts about maternal mortality in the past and how the problem might be tackled today. For example, the major causes of death for mothers in Britain prior to the thirties were similar to those found today among women in developing countries, most commonly haemorrhage and sepsis, though in Britain before the thirties, sepsis was a more common cause of death. The single biggest factor in the rapid decline in maternal mortality at the time was the introduction of antibiotics, followed by increased use of ergometrine and blood transfusion in case of haemorrhage, better training and better organization of obstetric care.

A study like this offers hope on the one hand that the advances in maternal healthcare made in developed

---

[12] Irvine Loudon, "Maternal Mortality in the Past and Its Relevance to Developing Countries Today", *American Journal of Clinical Nutrition* 72, no. 1 (July 2000), http://ajcn.nutrition.org/content/72/1/241s.full.

countries some eighty years ago could, using relatively low cost interventions, be replicated in other countries. On the other hand, a historical detail not commented upon in the paper serves as a warning against the received wisdom that the promotion of abortion will significantly reduce maternal mortality. It is quite clear from the evidence that maternal mortality was effectively tackled in Britain decades before the legalization of abortion. The lessons of history provide the first warning against the presumption that abortion is necessary to save women's lives.

The Abortion Lobby's Trojan Horse

This presumption remains very strong, so much so that an article in the respected *British Medical Journal* could glibly claim: "*Safe abortion is pro-life. Safe abortion saves lives. Just ask your grandmother.*"[13] It is difficult to imagine even raising the subject with my devoutly Catholic Maltese nanna, but one suspects her response, assuming she had even grasped what I meant, would have been to ask me if *Marija Santa* I had sold my soul to the devil.

I would argue that abortion is fundamentally a lifestyle not a health issue, and however one views abortion per se, we should stop talking as though it were treatment for an illness. It's very fashionable to say that "pregnancy isn't a disease, you know", and it certainly is not—abortion is therefore not a cure. Abortion continues to be touted as a women's health issue, from pro-abortion marches entitled "March for Women's Lives" to the emotive slogan

---

[13] Peter Saunders, "British Medical Journal Perpetuates Myths about Illegal Abortions", *Christian Medical Comment* (blog), 10 July 2012, http://pjsaunders .blogspot.co.uk/2012/07/british-medical-journal-perpetuates.html.

shouted at many a pro-life demonstration: "Right to life, that's a lie! You don't care if women die!" Marie Stopes International's past propaganda efforts in the field of abortion and contraception promotion have come under the seemingly compassionate label of "Make Women Matter." But if legal abortion really does save lives, one would at the very least expect to find that countries with permissive laws would tend to have the lowest rates of maternal death. Counter-intuitively perhaps, this does not appear to be the case.

A study on maternal health in Chile came to the conclusion that legal abortion is not a factor in reducing maternal mortality.[14] Chile is an interesting model for research into this area as abortion was banned in 1989, and if the alarmist claims of the international abortion lobby held water, one would expect to see a marked increase in deaths after that date. Far from there being an increase in maternal mortality in Chile, the maternal death rate has continued to decline and is now one of the lowest in Latin America.

The paper highlights the importance of interventions known to reduce maternal mortality rates. However, the study also examines the much-neglected subject of female education, noting that the risk of maternal death decreased with every year a woman spent in education. This paper is by no means the first to refute the abortion industry's major justification for the promotion of abortion in developing countries, and it is unlikely to be the last.

It should perhaps be noted at this point that at no point in this book do I include within the definition of abortion

---

[14] Elard Koch et al., "Women's Education Level, Maternal Health Facilities, Abortion Legislation and Maternal Deaths: A Natural Experiment in Chile from 1957–2007", *Public Library of Science*, 4 May 2012, http://journals.plos.org/plosone/article?id=10.1371/journal.pone.0036613.

situations such as ectopic pregnancy, where a doctor may be forced to intervene to save a woman's life and, in doing so, the life of the unborn baby may be lost along with part of the fallopian tube as a foreseen but unintended consequence of that intervention on the woman, nor would I include a woman with cancer undergoing chemotherapy to save her life which may have the consequence of ending the life of the unborn child who was not the target of the treatment. The abortion industry gains a great deal of ground by muddying the waters, and it is important in terms of the debate to ensure that there is no confusion when it comes to the difference between a direct, lethal assault on the unborn and a medical intervention that may have the foreseen but unintended consequence of ending an innocent life.

Unsafe Abortion

If abortion is no lifesaver, it does sometimes kill women, and it is the "unsafe abortion" argument that is being used most aggressively to promote abortion around the world. Britain's Department for International Development (DFID) uses unsafe abortion as its major line of defence in promoting and funding abortion. International organisations list "unsafe abortion" as one of the major causes of maternal death after haemorrhage and sepsis, but not only is this claim highly questionable; the category itself is misleading for a number of reasons.

First, when the overwhelming majority of people, including journalists and politicians, hear the word "abortion", they tend to think of induced abortion when the category of unsafe abortion can include deaths as a result of spontaneous abortion, otherwise known as miscarriage, giving a distorted picture of the number of women who are dying as a result of *induced abortion.*

It can be extremely difficult even for a trained doctor to determine whether a woman in the first trimester of pregnancy is experiencing life-threatening complications as a result of miscarriage or abortion. The symptoms are so similar that an online abortion group which sells pills to women in pro-life countries instructs women who suffer complications: "If you live in a place where abortion is a crime and you don't have a doctor you trust, you can still access medical care. You do not have to tell the medical staff that you tried to induce an abortion; you can tell them that you had a spontaneous miscarriage.... The symptoms are exactly the same and the doctor will not be able to see or test for any evidence of an abortion."[15] I will leave aside for the moment the rank hypocrisy of a pro-abortion organization artificially creating a backstreet abortion industry that they can then condemn. What is more worrying is the fact that women are encouraged to lie or withhold information to the people attempting to save them.

Second, we should be aware of the loaded use of "unsafe" here. The abortion lobby has been very successful in creating a false association between "safe" and "legal" abortion (a favourite line of pro-abortion politicians has until recently been that abortion should be "safe, legal and rare"), with the implication being that if abortion were only decriminalised in every country of the world, maternal deaths as a result of abortion would be virtually eliminated, but any medical procedure involves a level of risk, and abortion is no different.

[15] "How Do You Know If You Have Complications and What Should You Do?", Women on Web, accessed 12 February 2017, https://www .womenonweb.org/en/page/485/how-do-you-know-if-you-have -complications-and-what-should-you-do.

The 8 percent rate of maternal deaths in developed countries (where abortion is most likely to be legal) is the result of abortion complications.[16] South Africa has some of the most permissive abortion laws in the world. When the country experienced an increase in its already poor maternal mortality rate following the arrival of a UK-funded abortion organization, UN lobbyist Peter Smith commented: "It is farcical for the government to talk about safe abortions in situations without sterile surgical facilities, safe blood transfusion or emergency back-up. Running abortion clinics in slums, shanty towns and the bush will harm or kill women as well as killing babies."[17]

Women in Britain and women in South Africa have access to legal abortion, but in the end, a woman experiencing abortion complications in Britain can get emergency help within minutes—a woman living in an isolated settlement in South Africa cannot do so.

The term "safe abortion" is used synonymously with legal abortion and almost exclusively in terms of trying to promote legislative change. This is clear enough from the contradictory definitions given of what exactly constitutes an unsafe abortion. The WHO has written in the past:

> Abortions done outside the bounds of law are likely to be unsafe even if they are done by people with medical training.... Thus, as in previous efforts to estimate abortion incidence and consistent with WHO practice, we used

[16] United Nations Millennium Development Goals Gender Chart via UN Statistics Division, UN Women (2014), http://www.unwomen.org/-/media/headquarters/attachments/sections/library/publications/2014/gender%20gap%202014%20for%20web%20pdf.pdf?la=en.

[17] "UK Funding to Abort the Babies of the Poor Condemned by Pro-Life Group SPUC", Society for the Protection of Unborn Children, 4 January 2011, https://www.spuc.org.uk/news/press-releases/2011/january/uk-funding-to-abort-the-babies-of-the-poor-condemned-by-pro-life-group-spuc.

the operational definition of unsafe abortions, which is abortions done in countries with highly restrictive abortion laws, and those that do not meet legal requirements, in countries with less restrictive laws. Safe abortions were defined as those that meet legal requirements, in countries with liberal laws, or where the laws are liberally interpreted such that safe abortions are generally available.[18]

The legalistic understanding of safety is quite clear within such a definition, but elsewhere on the WHO website, unsafe abortion is defined as "a procedure for terminating an unwanted pregnancy either by persons lacking the necessary skills or in an environment lacking the minimal medical standards or both."[19] By that definition abortions that are particularly dangerous to women could well occur in countries with permissive abortion laws.

The June 2014 Department for International Development document "Safe and Unsafe Abortion" gives no clear definition at all, or indeed any definition, of what it understands to be safe abortion, even though DFID is at pains to support its provision—whatever it is.

A final point about the "unsafe abortion" argument. Abortion promoters have a record going back fifty years of wildly exaggerating or simply fabricating figures for deaths from illegal abortion. For example, in Britain during the 1960s it was suggested that, before the passing of the Abortion Act in 1967, there were as many as 100,000 or

[18] Lucia Muchova, "Analysis: WHO Staff Report Calls for Legal Abortion in Developing World, Abortion Figures Inflated", Center for Family & Human Rights, 2 February 2012, https://c-fam.org/friday_fax/analysis-who-staff-report-calls-for-legal-abortion-in-developing-world-abortion-figures-inflated/.

[19] World Health Organization, "Sexual and Reproductive Health, Preventing Unsafe Abortion", accessed 12 February 2017, http://www.who.int/reproductivehealth/topics/unsafe_abortion/hrpwork/en/.

even 250,000 backstreet abortions carried out every year. However, in 1966, the Royal College of Obstetricians and Gynaecologists stated that "these, and an earlier figure of 50,000, are without any secure factual foundation of which we are aware."[20]

Former abortionist and abortion campaigner Bernard Nathanson admitted that he deliberately deceived people about the number of abortion deaths in the United States. He candidly admitted:

> We aroused enough sympathy to sell our program of permissive abortion by fabricating the number of illegal abortions done annually in the U.S. The actual figure was approaching 100,000 but the figure we gave to the media repeatedly was 1,000,000. Repeating the big lie often enough convinces the public. The number of women dying from illegal abortions was around 200–250 annually. The figure constantly fed to the media was 10,000. These false figures took root in the consciousness of Americans convincing many that we needed to crack the abortion law.[21]

Abortion advocates continued to use Dr Nathanson's original figures in spite of his admission.

In 1982 it was claimed that 2,000 women died in Portugal every year as a result of illegal abortion. The figure was published in serious news reports even though the UN Demographic Yearbook found that only 2,099 women in their main childbearing years died from all causes in

[20] Ann Farmer, *By Their Fruits: Eugenics, Population Control and the Abortion Campaign* (Washington, D.C.: Catholic University of America Press, 2008), p. 203.

[21] Bernard Nathanson, "Confessions of an Ex-Abortionist", Catholic Education Resource Center, accessed 12 February 2017, http://www.catholic education.org/en/controversy/abortion/confessions-of-an-ex-abortionist.html.

Portugal during the year for which statistics were most recently available. Either Portugal had an extraordinary absence of fatal accidents and disease among younger women or the 2,000 figure was a pure fantasy.[22]

Dr Malcolm Potts, a neo-Malthusian abortion pioneer and former director of IPPF (International Planned Parenthood Federation), who has never as far as I am aware changed his mind on this subject, wrote in his book *Abortion*: "Those who want the law to be liberalized will stress the hazards of illegal abortion and claim that hundreds, or thousands, of women die unnecessarily each year, when the actual number is far lower."[23]

It is difficult, therefore, to avoid greeting with scepticism papers[24] making dramatic claims about unsafe abortion when they are produced by an organisation such as the Guttmacher Institute, which is ideologically committed to the legalization of abortion around the world. This is not to suggest that everything Guttmacher produces is inevitably false, but pro-abortion assumptions underlie so much of the research. Some of the Guttmacher authors have links with campaign groups such as the National Abortion Federation and Abortion Access Project. Unfortunately, Britain's Department for International Development, which should take a pragmatic view of what interventions are needed, appears content to fund studies that will yield up the answers it wants and to involve itself in the pursuit of the abortion agenda at the cost of women's lives.

---

[22] Robert Whelan, *Legal Abortion Examined: 21 Years of Abortion Statistics* (London, UK: SPUC Educational Research Trust, 1992).

[23] Malcolm Potts, *Abortion* (Cambridge: Cambridge University Press, 1977), p. 529.

[24] Gilda Sedgh et al., "Induced Abortion: Incidence and Trends Worldwide from 1995 to 2008", *Lancet* 379, no. 9816 (19 January 2012): 625–32; published online 19 January 2012, https://www.guttmacher.org/sites/default/files/pdfs/pubs/journals/Sedgh-Lancet-2012-01.pdf.

Because ironically, the promotion of abortion can be a killer of women in a much subtler and indirect way than by direct commission. Donna Harrison, president of the American Association of Pro-Life Obstetricians and Gynaecologists, has written: "It is scientifically, medically, and morally unacceptable to divert resources from interventions proven to reduce maternal mortality to the provision of abortion, under the guise of 'decreasing unsafe abortion'. The better way to reduce the human rights dimension of maternal mortality is to provide resources targeting the causes of 90 percent of maternal mortality."[25]

The Department for International Development and Its Friends

In Britain, there is a strong working relationship between DFID and pro-abortion research organisations. Besides the Guttmacher Institute, from which many of the statistics used by DFID originate, there are other research organs that are influencing public policy on abortion. *Options*,[26] with its neutral-sounding name, is a consultancy group founded by Dr Tim Black, who also co-founded Marie Stopes International. Not only is *Options* a wholly owned subsidiary of Marie Stopes International; the CEO of Marie Stopes International is chair of the board of directors of *Options*. DFID has commissioned *Options* to carry out research on a number of occasions, meaning that DFID's policy on abortion, contraception and maternal

[25] Quoted in George Mulcaire-Jones and Robert Scanlon, "Safe Passages: Pro-Life Response to the Tragedy of Maternal Deaths", *Linacre Quarterly* 78, no. 2 (May 2011): 204–5, http://www.aaplog.org/wp-content/uploads/2011/05/Safe-maternal-mortality.pdf.

[26] See their website at http://www.options.co.uk/our-history.

health is being shaped by data produced by a company owned by a major abortion provider. It is as absurd a situation as the British government asking an international fast-food chain to provide research to shape health policy on obesity.

The impact of such slanted research is quite clear, with or without transparency from DFID. The International Development Committee is appointed by the British House of Commons "to examine the expenditure, administration, and policy of the Department for International Development and its associated public bodies".[27] The committee's fifth report on maternal health, published in 2007–2008,[28] discusses at great length maternal mortality in developing countries and DFID's response to this tragedy. The report does include some discussion of practical ways to bring down the maternal death rate such as training skilled birth attendants and the need to educate and empower women more generally, but it is notable that in the entire report the deadliest complication (haemorrhage) is mentioned twice (once in the context of abortion), post-partum infection is mentioned twice (once in the context of abortion), obstructed labour gets two mentions, whilst abortion crops up seventy-one times. The International Development Committee's perverse obsession with abortion reemerged in a press release[29] in 2008, in which it falsely claimed that abortion is the third

[27] House of Commons International Development Committee, *Maternal Health: Fifth Report of Session 2007–08*, vol. I, 6 February 2008, http://www.publications.parliament.uk/pa/cm200708/cmselect/cmintdev/66/66i.pdf.

[28] Ibid.

[29] International Development Committee Announcement, New Publication: Maternal Health, "Up to One Million Mothers Dying Needlessly Each Year in Developing Countries", Parliament.UK, accessed 12 February 2017, http://www.parliament.uk/business/committees/committees-archive/international-development/indo708an28/.

biggest cause of maternal death. Opponents of abortion and contraception were also accused (minus evidence) of "effectively condemning millions of women a year to death or disability" whilst the committee failed seriously to question the number of women being condemned to die from sepsis or postpartum haemorrhage because international aid agencies are too obsessed with promoting abortion to put the necessary funds into safe childbirth.

Money spent on abortion is not going to lifesaving maternal health care and therefore represents an investment in death twice over. In other words, the Western obsession with promoting its own vision of sexuality onto the rest of the world is not only costing the lives of the unborn; it is costing the lives of women through neglect.

This is perhaps most obvious in the use of the Millennium Development Goals (MDGs) to justify the promotion of abortion and so-called "reproductive health". When the MDGs were first being promoted, SPUC (Society for the Protection of Unborn Children) raised concerns that there was a pro-abortion agenda in play. This was not a popular message when the Make Poverty History Campaign was in full swing and enjoyed the support of hundreds of organisations including many Catholic agencies. An article I penned for the *Pro-Life Times* warning of the pro-abortion agenda was angrily condemned as "completely untrue" by one Catholic agency, which apparently failed to notice the number of abortion organisations supporting Make Poverty History.

At the current time, little attempt is made to hide the fact that abortion is being promoted under the auspices of improving maternal health. As a paper produced by Guttmacher glibly claims: "Measures to reduce the incidence of unintended pregnancy and unsafe abortion, including investments in family planning services and safe abortion care, are crucial steps toward achieving the Millennium Development Goals."[30]

The Department for International Development is open about its determination to promote abortion around the world but has repeatedly refused to disclose the proportion of its maternal health funding that is being spent promoting and providing abortions. Andrew Mitchell, while Secretary of State for International Development, claimed that such information "cannot be provided without incurring disproportionate cost",[31] whilst Baroness Verma has stated in the House of Lords that whilst she could disclose that £186 million were spent over five years on maternal health initiatives and abortion provision, "it is not possible to disaggregate how much was spent on the latter two categories."[32]

Interestingly, Lord Laird asked many years ago exactly what "disproportionate cost" meant in relation to failing to provide a complete answer to a parliamentary question, to which he was told that it was a disproportionate cost if it would take in excess of £500 worth of staff hours.[33] I can only assume that parliamentary researchers get paid a lot more or work a great deal more slowly than I do.

This shyness about abortion data is all the more pointed when compared to the DFID's boastfulness about some other aspects of its spending. For example, DFID reported

[30] Sedgh et al., "Induced Abortion", p. 14.

[31] House of Commons Written Answers, "International Planned Parenthood Federation: Finance", 21 March 2011, Column 844W, https://publications.parliament.uk/pa/cm201011/cmhansrd/cm110321/text/110321w0003.htm.

[32] Written answers about abortion, question asked by Lord Alton of Liverpool, Parliament.UK, 25 January 2011, https://www.publications.parliament.uk/pa/ld201011/ldhansrd/text/110125w0001.htm#11012564000804

[33] Question answered by Lord Falconer of Thoroton, Parliament.UK, 24 May 2000, http://www.publications.parliament.uk/pa/ld199900/ldhansrd/vo000524/text/00524w05.htm.

buying 916,324 condoms for Rwanda[34] (the 916,325th man presumably didn't get one) and paying for more than 40,000 victims of sexual violence in Congo to receive treatment. But how many abortions? That is just too difficult, too costly to find out.

Abortion remains a sensitive and divisive issue, and in an era of supposed transparency and accountability, taxpayers surely have a right to know how much money is going to promoting abortion and precisely how it compares with the amount being spent saving the lives of women and babies.

Almost more revealing than the groups to whom DFID turns for data are the organisations with whom DFID chooses to work when it comes to the allocation of funding. DFID has given tens of millions of pounds' worth of funding to IPPF through various projects. IPPF is a major player in the promotion and provision of abortion around the world; the majority of IPPF's member associations provide abortion and abortion-related services, and IPPF's strategic plan for Africa has included an 82 percent increase in so-called "abortion services" with a target of over 270,000 by 2015.[35] This is whilst claiming publicly that IPPF "does not seek to 'increase' the number of abortions". According to IPPF's Annual Performance Report for 2010, it was responsible for half a million medical and surgical abortions.

[34] Department for International Development, *Annual Report and Accounts 2010–11, Volume 1: Annual Report* (Norwich: TSO, 7 July 2011), p. 55, http://www.dfid.gov.uk/Documents/publications1/departmental-report/2011/Annual-report-2011-vol1.pdf. I am indebted to former SPUC researcher Daniel Blackman for sharing this material with me.

[35] Peter Baklinski, "African Genocide: Planned Parenthood to Ramp Up African 'Abortion Services' by 82%", LifeSiteNews.com, 25 January 2012, http://www.lifesitenews.com/news/african-genocide-planned-parenthood-to-ramp-up-african-abortion-services-by.

IPPF speaks in messianic terms about its vision for the world: "Access is the gateway to the world of choice IPPF envisions" and "IPPF works towards a world in which women, men and young people everywhere have control over their own bodies, and therefore their destinies."[36] A woman haemorrhaging to death in childbirth has no destiny; an asphyxiated newborn will not grow up to enjoy this utopian world of which IPPF so wistfully dreams.

Another major recipient of UK funds is Marie Stopes International (MSI). The majority of MSI's considerable income comes from governmental reimbursements and fees for services including abortion and contraception provision.[37] DFID, through a Partnership Programme Agreement, has awarded MSI millions of pounds of taxpayers' money.[38] MSI has also received nearly £12 million for an MSI Global International Partnership which aimed to reduce fertility in Malawi.[39] MSI estimated that they provided 1.3 million abortion and postabortion procedures in 2010.

In one of their written responses to maternal death, Dr George Mulcaire-Jones and Robert Scanlon of Maternal Life International expose the hypocrisy of the abortion lobby with devastating eloquence:

> There remains a chasm between the villages of Africa and the cities of Geneva, Stockholm, London, and Washington,

---

[36] *Sexual Rights: An IPPF Declaration* (London: International Planned Parenthood Federation, 2008), https://www.ippf.org/sites/default/files/sexualrights ippfdeclaration_1.pdf.

[37] Ibid.

[38] DFID, "Maria Stopes International—PPA", 22 October 2012, http://www.gov.uk/guidance/programme-partnership-arrangements-ppas.

[39] DFID, "Giving Women a Choice in Malawi", 21 December 2010, https://www.gov.uk/government/case-studies/giving-women-a-choice-in-malawi.

D.C. It is the chasm representing the distance between a woman dying in a birthing hut without sanitation, running water, or hope, and the carpeted board rooms where strategies are developed and priorities assigned. Vast resources, which should have been directed to funding improvements in essential obstetrical care, have gone to a different agenda—so called "reproductive health." Rather than focus on the real causes and solutions to maternal mortality, Safe Motherhood has become entangled within a "reproductive rights" agenda, which emphasizes access to contraception and promotes abortion.[40]

Maternal mortality globally is in decline, and that is a cause for celebration. However, Dr Yoshihara of C-Fam has warned that there may well be a catch in those statistics. She makes the point in her own research that maternal deaths may be in decline but so are fertility rates, meaning that the proportion of pregnancies ending in the death of the mother may not in fact have changed as much as it would first appear. Statistically speaking, if fewer women are giving birth, fewer women are going to die, but to cite this as a victory is rather like saying "the number of people in Britain suffering from dementia has reduced rapidly in the last decade since we introduced compulsory euthanasia at seventy." For women who choose to have children, the risk may not have changed and may indeed be increasing. Dr Yoshihara writes:

For years the world's foremost aid agencies have made family planning the top priority in addressing maternal health, in an effort to further quash fertility. Medical interventions that actually address maternal health—such

[40] George Mulcaire-Jones and Robert Scanlon, "Safe Passages Pro-Life Response to the Tragedy of Maternal Deaths", *The Linacre Quarterly* 78:2 (2011): 203.

as skilled birth attendants and antenatal care—have been kicked down to second or third place on the funding list.

One reason is that agencies find it easier to dispense contraception than to overhaul far away health systems. Another is that they can measure "contraceptive prevalence" more easily than they can assess qualitative improvements in medical care. In an era of fiscal constraints and donor demands for accountability, particular agency interests drive funding priorities that may not make much medical sense.[41]

This is surely the chasm to which Dr Mulcaire-Jones is referring.

Childbirth is rendered safe by a range of entirely ethical solutions. There are mercifully few people alive on this planet who have a problem with making available to women such lifesaving interventions as antenatal monitoring, trained midwives, caesarean section, blood transfusion (and with it the ability to store blood safely), good sanitation and antibiotics. There is no reason why there should be this massive ideological battle going on over the bodies of dead women and babies. Until it ends, the body count can only continue to grow.

---

[41] Susan Yoshihara, "Friday Fax Analysis: Drop in Global Maternal Deaths Doesn't Mean Maternal Health Improving", Center for Family and Human Rights, 24 May 2012, https://c-fam.org/friday_fax/friday-fax-analysis-drop-in -global-maternal-deaths-doesnt-mean-maternal-health-improving/.

The Continuing Struggle for Equality

Men make the moral code and they expect women to accept it.
They have decided that it is entirely right and proper for men to
fight for their liberties and their rights, but that it is not right and
proper for women to fight for theirs.

— Emmeline Pankhurst

A Growing Backlash

There is an unhealthy temptation simply to dismiss feminism of all kinds out of hand or to suggest that is unnecessary or possibly that it was never necessary. I have watched
men walk out of my talks as soon as the word "feminism"
was mentioned or make a point of scowling at me all the
way through to express their disapproval. I have had well-
meaning individuals (to give humanity the benefit of the
doubt) attempt to convince me during Q&A sessions that
I don't really believe we need all this feminist stuff when
there are such lovely strong women like myself already
involved with the movement.

Among women (and arguably men) there can be an
anxiety about associating with an ideology that has for so
many years been characterised as antireligion, antimar-
riage, antinatalist and hostile in every other sense to values

Emmeline Panhurt, *My Own Story* (1914, Project Gutenberg, 2011), p. 268,
http://www.gutenberg.org/files/34856/34856-h/34856-h.htm.

cherished by millions of women around the world. It is still quite common to hear women disassociating themselves from feminism with "I'm not a feminist but I'm really worried about ..."

However, participating in a backlash—and there has been a backlash against feminism in the West—is not an answer in a world where the status of women remains unacceptable in many countries including our own. We should not delude ourselves that women enjoy the level of protection and equality to which they are entitled in spite of the real advances of the last eighty years in some areas. If that statement appears a little questionable, it might be worth considering a few aspects of life in which women are significantly or uniquely at risk whilst their experiences are not always taken seriously or reported accurately.

Rape

In Britain, according to Rape Crisis UK, the conviction rate for rape is lower than for any other crime, suggesting that the overwhelming majority of rapists are never punished for their crimes.[1] This is not to say that there have not been significant improvements in the way rape is handled by both the police and the courts. The treatment of women who report rape has come a long way since the '80s fly-on-the-wall documentary *Police* showed male officers rudely dismissing a distressed woman's allegation of gang rape, provoking questions in Parliament and quiet changes in the way the police responded to rape cases.

[1] "Rape Crisis England & Wales Headline Statistics 2015–16", Rape Crisis England and Wales, accessed 12 February 2017, http://rapecrisis.org.uk /statistics.php.

The 2015 Office of National Statistics report on crime in England and Wales[2] noted a substantial increase in reports of sexual offences but cautioned that this is most likely to be a result of better recording and greater willingness on the part of victims to come forward than a sudden increase in the number of cases. To put Britain's experience into context, however, in South Africa the number of rapes work out at around 147 a day,[3] with higher instances of rape-associated violence and gang rape, alongside considerably greater reluctance by victims to seek help.

Campaigners rightly express concern that when cases are reported in the press, the level of sympathy to which a victim is entitled tends to be determined by her social status—the young mother, the vicar's daughter, the doctor's wife—not the severity of the crime to which she has been subjected. Conversely, some of the most notorious sexual predators are glorified in the public imagination— Jack the Ripper's name has been leant to cocktails; he has been the subject of books, films, songs and tourist walks where people can visit the places he murdered women.[4] Why should such a despicable man be treated as a legend when his only known achievement was as a sadistic—and elusive—serial killer?

An objector put it to me once that the only reason there are so many reports of rape is because more and more

<hr>

[2] "Crime in England and Wales: Year Ending September 2015", no. 7, "Sexual Offences", Office for National Statistics, 21 January 2016, http://www.ons.gov.uk/peoplepopulationandcommunity/crimeandjustice/bulletins/crimeinenglandandwales/yearendingseptember2015#sexual-offences.

[3] "Prevalence", Rape Crisis: Cape Town Trust, accessed 12 February 2017, http://rapecrisis.org.za/rape-in-south-africa/#prevalence.

[4] Mary Ann Nichols et al., "Can You Name the Victims of Jack the Ripper?", *Huffington Post*, 8 June 2016, http://www.huffingtonpost.co.uk/ending-victimisation-and-blame/jack-the-ripper_b_7946984.html.

women are lying about it, but this is a difficult point to support unless one goes by the assumption that women are by nature more prone to dishonesty than men. According to the Crown Prosecution Service's report into perverting the course of justice, false allegations of rape are rare, and only a minority of false allegations that are made are malicious.[5]

Rape should not be yet another female nightmare to fall through the feminist/antifeminist fault line. It has been very clear to me when sifting through the thousands of commentaries, opinion pieces, rants in comboxes and assorted unsolicited private messages on the subject, that any attempt to blame women for rape is on some level an attack on men in general. I am by no means the only feminist to have noticed that the persistent culture of blame that sees women as in some way "asking for it" through their behaviour, dress or alleged foolishness is also an attack on male behaviour. It presupposes that all men are potential rapists who may be tempted to assault a woman if they see too much of her figure or come across a pretty girl walking unchaperoned after dark. The majority of men are perfectly capable of appreciating female beauty or sexual allure without feeling the overwhelming urge to commit a violent crime. The notion that women have to protect themselves from rape (and by extension to protect men from their own base urges) feeds into both the age-old lie that women are to blame for their own misfortune and an antimale prejudice that sees the male population as ravenous animals with uncontrollable sex drives.

[5] Alison Levitt, "Charging Perverting the Course of Justice and Wasting Police Time in Cases Involving Allegedly False Rape and Domestic Violence Allegations", *Joint Report to the Director of Public Prosecutions*, March 2013, http://www.cps.gov.uk/publications/research/perverting_course_of_justice _march_2013.pdf.

Domestic Violence and Forced Marriage

In Britain, two woman are killed as a result of domestic violence every week on average, and globally, it is estimated that one in three women experience violence during their lifetimes. Domestic abuse can have a long-lasting effect on the physical and mental health of the adult on the receiving end, but also on the children of the household who, in the overwhelming majority of cases, either witness violence when it takes place or are located nearby.[6]

A paper published in the *Lancet* in 2014 warned not just about the risks of physical and sexual violence but also about practices such as female genital mutilation, which is thought to have been performed on between 100 and 140 million women and girls worldwide with over double that number at risk.[7] When William Cash MP spoke during a parliamentary debate[8] about visiting a hostel for abuse victims in India, he described being introduced to the woman in charge who had been beaten almost to death a total of eighteen times trying to protect other women. It is obscene in the twenty-first century that abuse like that should be regarded as an occupational hazard of being a woman protecting other women, but even those committed to raising awareness about such atrocities must beware of their own unwitting reinforcement of stereotypes. Violence against women was described during that

[6] "Domestic Violence—The Facts", Refuge, accessed 12 February 2017, http://www.refuge.org.uk/get-help-now/what-is-domestic-violence/domestic-violence-the-facts/.

[7] Mary Ellsberg et al., "Prevention of Violence against Women and Girls: What Does the Evidence Say?", *Lancet*, 20 November 2014, http://blogs.lshtm.ac.uk/samegroup/files/2014/11/Paper-1.pdf.

[8] *House of Commons Official Report: Parliamentary Debates (Hansard)*, vol. 573, no. 106, 17 January 2017, http://www.publications.parliament.uk/pa/cm201314/cmhansrd/chan106.pdf.

very parliamentary debate as "a global pandemic", but the word was ill-chosen. Violence is no such thing. It is not an illness; it is somebody's bad choice. It is no more an uncontrollable part of the human condition as rape, nor is it impossible to protect women (and men in some cases) from the horrors of domestic abuse if the political will exists to do so.

A similar linguistic lapse occurred in media reports of the horrific murder of an eight-year-old girl in Yemen.[9] Various media outlets described her as a "child bride" who died "at the hands of her husband" on her "wedding night" of massive internal injuries. She was a victim of a forced marriage, but by repeatedly using language such as "bride", "husband" and "wedding night", reporters inadvertently played into the hands of proponents of such unions and sanitised the true horror of what actually occurred. An eight-year-old girl was effectively sold by her family to a man in his forties who raped her to death. To grace the disgusting crime that brought about an innocent child's death as anything resembling a legitimate marriage insults her memory and softens the true nature of the atrocity committed.

The unnamed Yemeni child represents the 1.5 million girls under the age of fifteen who are handed over to older men around the world each year. One in nine girls in developing countries are married by the age of fifteen.[10] In 2016 Britain's Forced Marriage Unit gave assistance in 1,428 possible cases, but studies suggest that around three

[9] "8-Year-Old Yemeni Child Dies at Hands of 40-Year-Old Husband on Wedding Night", *Al Bawaba*, 9 September 2013, http://www.albawaba.com /editorchoice/yemen-child-marriage-human-rights-519066.

[10] Jimmy Carter, "Patriarchy and Violence against Women and Girls", *Lancet*, 20 November 2014, http://www.acesconnection.com/fileSendAction /fcType/o/fcOid/409721608759443561/filePointer/409721608759443715 /fodoid/409721608759443705/carter-2014.pdf.

thousand and four thousand forced marriages are thought to occur in Britain every year.[11] However, Nazir Afzal of the Crown Prosecution Service has been quoted in Parliament as stating that the true figure may be in the order of ten thousand cases a year.

As with so many issues facing women, there is room for hope, as the rate of child marriage shows signs of being in decline,[12] but the decline is so slow that by 2050 seven hundred million under-fifteens will have been forcibly married if the rate of progress does not accelerate.[13]

The World's Oldest Profession?

A more visible form of female exploitation is still ludicrously labelled "the world's oldest profession" (though I am fairly sure men were trading woolly mammoth burgers before they were trading in human flesh). Prostitution has always been treated with a mixture of disgust and fascination, but only towards the end of the twentieth century have powerful elements within the mainstream media begun to portray prostitution as enjoyable and even empowering for women. The notorious *Secret Diary of a Call Girl* was condemned as "seriously pernicious"[14] in

[11] Foreign & Commonwealth Office, *Forced Marriage Unit Annual Statistics 2016*, 9 March 2017, https://www.gov.uk/government/uploads/system/uploads/attachment_data/file/597869/Forced_Marriage_Unit_statistics-_2016.pdf.

[12] Anita Raj, Lotus McDougal and Melanie L. A. Rusch, "Changes in Prevalence of Girl Child Marriage in South Asia", *JAMA* 307, no. 19 (16 May 2012): 2027–29, http://jama.jamanetwork.com/article.aspx?articleid=1157484.

[13] "Ending Child Marriage: Progress and Prospects", UNICEF, 2014, http://www.unicef.org/media/files/Child_Marriage_Report_7_17_LR.pdf.

[14] "TV Hall of Shame: #2 Secret Diary of a Call Girl", *Guardian, TV&Radio Blog*, accessed 12 February 2017, http://www.theguardian.com/tv-and-radio/tvandradioblog/2011/feb/09/secret-diary-of-a-call-girl.

the *Guardian* and "not just wrong-headed but fundamentally dishonest"[15] in the *Telegraph*'s review for trying to sell prostitution as positive, romantic and safe, but *Call Girl* was no more irresponsible or dishonest than the cult TV drama *Sherlock* in this regard. In one episode, *A Scandal in Belgravia*, we are introduced to Irene Adler, Conan Doyle's high-society mistress updated to suit twenty-first century tastes as a dominatrix. From start to finish, Irene is portrayed as ferociously independent, wealthy, glamorous, articulate and—well, domineering. At one point, she is seen drugging and beating the helpless Sherlock Holmes with a riding crop—one does not get the sense that this is a woman to be trifled with. But besides the fact that the entire image of independence falls down when she is forced to plead to a man for help and eventually be rescued by him, the premise itself is deeply flawed. Ultimately, Irene Adler is a woman who is involved with an industry that is exploitative and dangerous, rendering herself vulnerable to injury, disease and violent death. The fact that she is a dominatrix, rather than acting out a more vulnerable role, does not alter the demeaning nature of the life she is living.

The media does not just send out dishonest messages about female exploitation through the world of drama. In its 2004 programme *Can Condoms Kill?* attacking the late Cardinal Trujillo, BBC Panorama filmed a legal brothel in the United States in which the prostitutes were referred to as "professionals" being carefully looked after by a madame in a business suit. The implication was that these women had made a career choice like any other, enjoyed being prostitutes and were very much in control of the situation.

---

[15] Gerard O'Donovan, "Secret Diary of a Call Girl, ITV2, Review", 28 January 2010, http://www.telegraph.co.uk/culture/tvandradio/7095052/Secret -Diary-of-a-Call-Girl-ITV2-review.html.

This myth appears to have been swallowed by Amnesty International, a once highly respected campaigning organisation which used to focus its energies on freeing political prisoners and ending torture. In December 2013, Amnesty circulated a paper[16] putting the case for decriminalising prostitution on the grounds that laws prohibiting prostitution are based on "a naïve view of sex workers as victims which denies the possibility that they have made a legitimate choice in engaging in this work. It is a mistake to believe that all sex work is a form of forced labour."[17] The paper states: "Amnesty International is opposed to the criminalisation or punishment of activities related to the buying or selling of consensual sex between adults.... The criminalization of voluntary sex between adults, whether for direct monetary gain or otherwise, threatens the rights to health, nondiscrimination, equality, privacy, and security of person. In addition, the right to freely chosen gainful work (Article 6, ICESCR) may be jeopardized by the criminalization of sex work."

Amnesty did, however, acknowledge the "imperfect" contexts which might lead a woman to the gainful work of selling her body on a street corner. As columnist Julie Bindel[18] responded: " 'Imperfect' is one way of describing a trade built on physical abuse, rape, child sex abuse, sadism and greed. It is highly offensive of Amnesty to pretend that this is similar to other industries. In what

[16]"Decriminaliazation of Sex Work: Policy Background Document", *Amnesty Prostitution Policy Document*, accessed 12 February 2017, https://www.scribd.com/doc/202126121/Amnesty-Prostitution-Policy-document.

[17]"Breaking Free Opposes Amnesty International's Call to Legalize Prostitution", Breaking Free, accessed 12 February 2017, http://www.breakingfree.net/files/breakingfree/files/amnestyinternationalstatement.pdf.

[18]Julie Bindel, "An Abject Inversion of Its Own Principles", *Daily Mail*, 23 January 2014, http://www.dailymail.co.uk/news/article-2544983/JULIE-BINDEL-An-abject-inversion-principles.html#ixzz2ruyWhFcZ.

other job do the occupational hazards include beatings, theft of earnings, sexually transmitted diseases, unwanted pregnancies, forcible removal of children, constant threats and even death?"

A documentary about women who had escaped prostitution entitled *Not for Sale*[19] exposed the industry in all its squalid colours, with former prostitutes describing the many harrowing encounters they had had and the degrading acts they had been expected to perform. One woman said frankly that she had not woken up one morning and thought, "Ooooh the sex industry. That sounds like a really great career choice." The fact is that if prostitution were the gainful, freely chosen employment that certain sectors of society wish to believe it is, there would be recruitment drives at local job centres, school career departments would surely include a "sex work" stall at their career fairs and parents would do everything possible to help their daughters achieve that burning ambition to go on the game. Few truly believe that prostitution is a positive choice for any woman.

Studies (largely ignored by the media and misguided campaigning groups) report that the overwhelming majority of prostitutes want to get out, are drug-dependent and have been the victims of violent assault and rape. Far from this being a consensual practice between two adults, the average age of entry into prostitution is between twelve and fourteen years old, three-quarters of prostitutes are controlled by a pimp and the majority suffer from post-traumatic stress disorder.[20]

---

[19] European Women's Lobby and the Coalition Against Trafficking in Women, *Not for Sale* (2006), video, 23 min., https://www.womenlobby.org /EWL-campaign-clip-Not-for-sale-2006-EWL-CATW.
[20] "Breaking Free Opposes Amnesty International's Call to Legalize Prostitution".

A thirty-year study in the United States[21] concluded that few prostitutes die from natural causes and the leading cause of death was homicide; other causes included drugs, HIV and suicide, meaning that prostitution is the most dangerous situation in which women can find themselves. And our society, led by our media, increasingly encourages and exalts this practice.

Trafficking

None of these figures include women who are sold across Europe by traffickers in a modern form of slavery. The majority of victims of modern-day trafficking are women and children, and it is estimated that there are over twelve million people trapped in some form of slavery today, more than there were in the nineteenth century.[22] The West has been woefully slow in coming to terms with the evils of human trafficking, and opportunities continue to be lost to help those caught up in this trade.

A study of trafficked women in the United States threw up some awkward questions.[23] One of the most important findings of the study was that the overwhelming majority of women caught up in trafficking had contact with the medical profession, with well over half attending a healthcare clinic, often a Planned Parenthood clinic. Virtually all

---

[21] John J. Potterat et al., "Mortality in a Long-term Open Cohort of Prostitute Women", *American Journal of Epidemiology* 159, no. 8 (15 April 2004): 778–85, http://aje.oxfordjournals.org/content/159/8/778.full.

[22] United Nations Human Rights, Office of the High Commissioner, "Who Are the Victims of Human Trafficking?", 5 November 2009, http://www.ohchr.org/EN/NewsEvents/Pages/VictimsOfHumanTrafficking.aspx.

[23] "Health Consequences of Sex Trafficking", *Annals of Health Law* 23 (2014): 87, http://www.annalsofhealthlaw.com/annalsofhealthlaw/vol_23_issue_1?pg=94#pg95.

exhibited some symptoms of mental illness—depression, anxiety, "total mental devastation" as the study describes it—and physical injury, usually to the head and face, was common to the majority of trafficked women. It raises the question, why are these women slipping through the net? Why are they not being given the means necessary to escape? I am prepared to accept that overworked doctors may find it difficult to identify a trafficking victim if they do not know what they are looking for and do not expect to have one turning up in their consulting room, but considering the state many of these women are in when they seek medical help—suffering from STIs (sexually transmitted infections), pregnant, visibly physically injured, nervous, depressed, often shadowed by a much older man—it should surely ring alarm bells with those treating them.

It is particularly concerning when over half of all trafficking victims interviewed for this study had been through abortion, nearly a third had had multiple abortions and over half of the women said that they were forced. According to one campaigner, it is not at all uncommon for a pimp to take things into his own hands when a girl gets pregnant and to beat her into a miscarriage, but the figures I am citing do not include those incidents. Almost all the abortions cited were carried out at registered facilities, with Planned Parenthood cited in particular because, as one respondent put it, "they don't ask any questions." That respondent also pointed out that some of her six abortions were performed by an abortion doctor who was described as one of her clients (I would describe him as one of her pimp's clients), who illegally performed the abortions out of hours without recording them. He not only covered up the evidence of other men's abuse of this woman but also quite possibly his own. If an abortion facility performs an abortion on a trafficking victim—no questions asked—the staff of that facility are colluding directly in the enslavement of women.

Women as Sex Objects

Even in the apparent comfort and safety of the mainstream media, women continue to be relegated to the role of sex object. Images of women of an increasingly sexualised nature are used routinely in advertising campaigns to sell everything from cars to fruit juice. Every time a photograph of a semi-clad woman is used to sell a product, it perpetuates the notion that women are mere objects who exist to fulfil male desires. What is particularly insidious about this tendency is the fact that it is so rarely seen as insulting to women, who are expected to be grateful that they are being liberated from starchy, old-fashioned stereotypes. There is no older stereotype of a woman than as a sex object; we have simply lost our sense that there is anything wrong with this particular stereotype, or even that it is one.

In a society struggling to come to terms with the evil of paedophilia, the sexualisation of women in the media starts when girls have barely reached adolescence, with girls in their early teens portrayed as impossibly beautiful, svelte and erotic. Canadian charity MediaSmart acknowledges the advances in portrayals of women and girls in some areas but also warns of the detrimental effect on teenage girls who are "bombarded with images of sexuality, often dominated by stereotypical portrayals of women and girls as powerless, passive victims".[24]

[24] "Media and Girls", MediaSmarts, accessed 12 February 2017, http://mediasmarts.ca/gender-representation/women-and-girls/media-and-girls.

The unintentional misogyny surrounding the parading of the female body for advertising purposes creeps into the most unexpected fields, including the realm of public health awareness, where the motive may be well-intentioned but grossly insensitive all the same. Some years ago there was a breast-cancer awareness campaign which featured a female celebrity having her breasts fondled from behind by a male TV presenter. It was clearly intended as a light-hearted, slightly cheeky introduction to the subject of breast cancer, but all it did was to mock an extremely distressing ordeal faced by a significant proportion of the female population. There is nothing cheeky or sexy about breast cancer simply because it involves a woman's breasts. If we compare that approach to the terrifyingly ominous campaign about heart attack that the British Heart Foundation put out in 2008, the difference is immediately obvious. A clock face smashes, symbolising the failing heart; a man is seen fighting for breath as a viper slithers around his arm to demonstrate the feelings of constriction experienced during a cardiac episode. An actor scowls into the camera, warning against delaying calling an ambulance. But then, heart attack does not involve a sexualised part of the body, and it disproportionately affects men.

As has already been noted, the admonition "Please! There are ladies present!" or "We are in mixed company, gentlemen!" sounds gloriously antiquated to the modern ear and is anathema to many feminists. It feels a little too much like the phrase "not in front of the children", a misguided attempt at sheltering and protecting women from the rudeness, lewdness and general ickiness of male life (though having been the only female in the room whilst men have discussed penis extensions, this feminist would not mind awfully if the male of the species kept certain subjects to themselves).

The jury is out on the acceptability of chivalry more generally, but it is hard to see signs of progress in the contemporary trend to make casual sexual insults against women in public and in the media. No member of the liberal elite would awkwardly mutter "not in front of the ladies" in sophisticated, mixed company today, but shouting the c-word at a woman at a pro-life vigil is not regarded as beyond the pale. In 2009, on the BBC television show *Have I Got News for You*, a member of the then shadow Tory cabinet referred to a young woman as a "silly bitch" for saying that marriage was between a man and a woman, and there was very little criticism of his behaviour. There was some outcry that he suggested he might murder her, so women can be thankful for small mercies. Insulting women who express the wrong opinions is acceptable, but the BBC has not quite stooped to promoting femicide as yet.

Flippancy aside, however, there is something extremely distasteful about a senior politician behaving in such a way on a show produced by one of the most respected broadcasters in the world. In a society in which women's opinions are taken seriously, one might expect rigorous and sometimes heated debate, but a reference to a woman's alleged moral turpitude should be as unacceptable as use of the N-word.

I am not attempting to argue that there is a huge conspiracy going on in the media to undermine women in the name of feminism. When it comes to the media portrayal of women and female experience, it seems to me that much of the misogynistic undercurrent is unintentional, but it persists because society has become complacent and even arrogant about its treatment of women. It is so often in the name of promoting positive images of women that this misogyny rises to the surface; we are too pleased with ourselves, too certain of our own narrative—namely, that women have always been oppressed, but over a period of a hundred years or so the status of women has continued and will continue to improve. We are on the march towards progress. We may well be marching broadly in the right direction as the improvements in the status of women in some areas bears witness, but it is still possible that we have taken in a few wrong turns and cul-de-sacs en route.

It has been noted by feminists including Germaine Greer that women are still poorly represented in the media, tend to be identified by their status (particularly their marital status) and are disproportionately portrayed as passive, such as the victims of crime. However, the increasingly common stereotype of the strong woman is equally a symptom of a society which fails to appreciate the female genius. The sort of woman to which I refer can be found on the set of a James Bond or Dr Who production: glamorous, sexy and devastatingly beautiful (since women have to be sexually alluring to be worthy of any attention) but also quick-witted, articulate and brave. So far so good, it might appear. But look a little closer and the apparent strength counts for very little. Characters such as Amy Pond and Clara Oswald in Dr Who are typical of this stereotype. They are portrayed as sassy and independent (within the limitations of a supporting role), but beyond the snarky banter they are two-dimensional and shallow. Strong female characters are permitted to fit within a well-worn role of feistiness but are still not entitled to be complex, cultured, sensitive and intellectual. The hot-tempered, motor-mouthed woman is a stereotype dating back centuries. Neither society nor the media have yet found the courage to embrace and accept the multifaceted woman.

Violinists, Hijackers and the Right to Bodily Integrity

Over himself, over his body and mind, the individual is sovereign.

—John Stewart Mill, *On Liberty*

My Body, My Life, My Right to Decide

Partly as a result of socio-economic change but perhaps also because the "bundle of cells" argument has been lost, the central tenet of the abortion argument is currently the woman's right to control over her own body. Virtually every pro-abortion slogan alludes to this in some way: "My body, my life, my right to decide"; "Women should decide their fate, not the Church and not the State"; "Keep your rosaries off my ovaries!"; "Hands off my uterus!"; "My body not yours!" As I have already argued, a woman's right to choose has become a central point of feminist dogma, chanted ad nauseam like a mantra as though the statement were beyond question. But no statement, political or otherwise, should ever be regarded as beyond question or at least beyond rigorous analysis.

It is doubtful whether the early feminists would recognise slogans as self-centred and inward-looking as "*my* body, *my* life, *my* right to decide". As a pro-life feminist, the rhetoric at work in these statements of ownership comes across as embarrassingly childish—more reminiscent of a toddler stamping her foot and shouting "Mine!" than a grown woman embracing her empowerment.

Beneath the self-obsessed jargon, however, the assertion that women (and men for that matter) have a right to bodily integrity is hardly unreasonable, and the overwhelming majority of people across the political spectrum would uphold this belief. The right to bodily integrity is fundamental to many other rights such as the right to be protected from violence, rape, from unwanted or burdensome medical treatment; the right to bodily integrity informs the behaviour of the police, the penal system, the medical profession and the teaching profession.

Inevitably, the freedom to make fundamental choices about one's body includes the likelihood that individuals will make ill-judged decisions or simply decisions with which others may disagree. For example, if my friend is diagnosed with terminal cancer and finds, after several courses of life-prolonging chemotherapy, that she cannot cope with the side effects of the treatment any longer and wishes to stop even though it will result in a rapid hastening of her death, I may well disagree with her doing so. I may be desperate for her to continue treatment for as long as possible, but in the end, I cannot take her suffering from her, and it is not my business to tell her how much treatment she should be capable of enduring. I would have to respect her decision to discontinue treatment whether or not I thought that decision was right.

A more difficult case might involve an activist going on hunger strike who, after weeks of refusing food, becomes so weak and undernourished that he is at risk of death. The obvious solution, medically speaking, to save his life would be tube-feeding, but the hunger striker refuses to cooperate. However dangerous his situation and however much others might disagree with his actions, it would arguably be necessary to respect his decision even if it meant that he died needlessly as a result, if the only alternative were invasive force-feeding.

Whereas the pro-life movement has traditionally been very successful in discussing the humanity of the unborn child, over nearly fifty years of impassioned debate, very little has been done to address this most central of tenets—the right to bodily integrity—other than to recast the debate by reminding society of the right to life of the unborn child. The need to make a stand on behalf of the unborn child cannot be exaggerated in a society where the compelling scientific evidence of the unborn child's humanity is still ignored. However, I do not believe that hearts and minds can ever be fully changed on abortion if we avoid discussion of the pregnant woman's status head-on. Indeed, this may prove to be the most significant contribution pro-life feminism can make to the debate.

Absolute Sovereignty

"The only purpose for which power can be rightfully exercised over any member of a civilized community, against his will, is to prevent harm to others. His own good, either physical or moral, is not a sufficient warrant," declared John Stuart Mill in his *On Liberty*, in one of the most influential essays on liberty ever written. "Over himself, over his body and mind, the individual is sovereign." An individual's absolute sovereignty over his body is presupposed in any discussion on ethics, but the right to bodily integrity is not the same as an absolute right to do *anything* to one's own body, however harmful it might be to the individual concerned. Contrary to popular belief, no person has a legal right to do exactly what he wants with his own body, precisely because the acknowledgement of "absolute sovereignty" would constitute an attack on human rights. Human rights are inviolable and *inalienable*. Therefore, a person cannot alienate himself from his fundamental rights even if he chooses to do so, because to do so would be to jeopardise the rights of others. There are certain rights that cannot be signed away: a person cannot legitimately sign his own death warrant, for example, or sign a contract submitting to torture.

Former Canadian radio star Jian Ghomeshi[1] justified his fondness for sadism with the claim that these acts were consensual, and that there was nothing wrong with him beating up women for sexual satisfaction because they had agreed to the assault. Ghomeshi was eventually acquitted of multiple counts of sexual assault, but it was pointed out in the press that what Ghomeshi did was still immoral and *illegal* because assault is ipso facto a crime and a person cannot therefore legally consent to assault. Even in cases where the proposed act is not illegal, an individual may still not have a right to carry it out. For example, in Britain, suicide was decriminalised in the 1960s. Suicide was not established as a right; it was simply accepted that people who attempt suicide require help not punishment. Strenuous attempts are made in Britain and elsewhere to prevent suicide, from limiting the number of paracetamol an individual can purchase at any one time to the placing of safety nets and barriers around popular suicide spots such as bridges and tall buildings. Aiding and abetting suicide remains a serious criminal offence.

[1] Ashifa Kassam, "Jian Ghomeshi Acquitted of All Charges in Sexual Assault Trial", *Guardian*, 24 March 2016, http://www.theguardian.com/world/2016/mar/24/jian-ghomeshi-acquitted-sexual-assault-trial.

Sovereignty over the body is limited even where there is no question of another life being directly harmed as in abortion because ultimately, even if it were possible (which it is not) to argue that no rights are inalienable or inviolable, it is difficult to conceive of a situation in which serious harm to self would not indirectly harm others. If a person consents to being assaulted, this may well encourage sexual violence and leave others vulnerable to non-consensual acts; if a person commits suicide, others will be damaged by the act, whether it be the family and friends of the suicide or the individual who stumbles upon the dead body. John Stuart Mill's statement, in effect, refers to an impossible hypothesis, one in which a person's actions against himself cannot have an impact upon another.

Parasites, Hijackers and Predators

In the context of abortion, the right of a woman to control her own body increasingly focuses on a negative rather than a positive right, the right to be protected from the unborn child. Rather than dismissing the unborn as a bundle of cells, the unborn child is cast as the villain of the drama, very much alive, from whose dangerous influence the pregnant woman must be rescued. In order to sustain such an argument, the unborn becomes either a parasite, a hijacker or—at the extreme end of autonomy rhetoric— a predator. The entirely natural, millennia-old process of conceiving and bearing offspring is twisted beyond recognition into a war in which the woman's body is invaded and colonised by an aggressor.

The argument that the unborn is a parasite is common, but it is easily dismissed, as the term "parasite" has a very specific meaning. A parasite is of a different species to the "host", and the rules of biogenesis make it clear that no organism gestating within the body of its mother can therefore be labelled a parasite; the unborn child is precisely where, biologically, it is meant to be.

The hijacker argument, though more extreme, has considerably more currency than it deserves due to the influence of the "violinist on life support" analogy, which continues to be used to justify the violent termination of a pregnancy. The analogy imagines a person waking up to discover that a group of music lovers have abducted him and rigged him up as life support for a famous violinist. If he unplugs himself, the violinist will die. Whilst the analogy provides an interesting exploration of the relationship between pregnant woman and unborn child and asks pertinent questions about the extent to which a pregnant woman has a duty to carry a baby to term, it fails in the same way as the parasite analogy. In the majority of cases, pregnancy occurs as a result of a consensual and deliberate act which is in no way analogous to a person suddenly waking up to discover that he has been a victim of violence; the use of a human being as life support to another adult in the way suggested by the violinist analogy is an example of extraordinary and wholly unethical behaviour—human beings are not designed to be plugged into another person's cardiovascular system in this way. In the end, the unborn child is not a stranger to the mother in the way that the famous violinist is to the source of life support, and the analogy leaves no room to consider whether a parent has greater responsibilities towards his child than to a complete stranger, especially considering the fact that the needs of the unborn child are hardly unusual or unreasonable.

The most extreme argument in favour of abortion to protect the right to bodily integrity sees the unborn child of an unwanted pregnancy as a predator akin to a rapist, who invades and violates the female body through its un-welcome presence in the woman's uterus. In this scenario, the unborn child is granted a level of consciousness and culpability of which it is entirely incapable—a violent intruder or rapist knows what he is doing and is likely to know that what he is doing is morally reprehensible. Camille Paglia's take on the "unborn baby as aggressor" argument is to see abortion as a weapon against "pagan nature" itself which insists upon women being nurturers of new life: "Women inspired by the Uranian Aphrodite to produce spiritual progeny should view abortion as a sword of self-defense put into their hands by Ares, the war god. Government, guaranteeing freedom of religion, has no right to interfere in our quarrel with our Creator, in this case pagan nature. Under the carnal constitution that precedes social citizenship, women have the right to bear arms. The battlefield is internal and it belongs to us."[2]

What these three approaches to the unborn child in the context of bodily integrity have in common is a failure to address the fact that unlike a parasite, hijacker or predator, the unborn child belongs in the woman's uterus and argu-ably has a right to be there; the uterus is designed for the specific purpose of gestating and protecting the unborn child. Only by taking the view Paglia appears to espouse, that a woman should be in a permanent state of warfare against her own body rather than in its defence, is it pos-sible to take these approaches to the unborn seriously. Even then, the only option suggested by such a belief is to embrace a form of continuous human sacrifice as the price of female empowerment.

What these flawed arguments also highlight is the impos-sibility of creating an appropriate analogy to pregnancy.

[2] Camille Paglia, *Vamps and Tramps* (New York: Vintage Books, 1994), p. 41.

The symbiotic relationship between mother and child within pregnancy is unique and cannot be compared with any other relationship or human interaction. The failure to acknowledge the uniqueness of mammalian reproduction represents a serious flaw in the pro-abortion argument for absolute autonomy.

Pro-Life Feminism and the Right to Bodily Integrity

It is necessary for pro-life feminists to challenge the zeitgeist in which pregnancy is viewed as a form of female enslavement (both pro-abortion and pro-life activists use the analogy of slavery in their arguments) but also to dispel the myth that to be pro-life is to view women as walking human incubators whose sole purpose in life is to sustain and raise children. Just as no sane person asks a pregnant woman when her fetus is due or whether she has thought of a name for her pregnancy tissue, it is difficult to imagine a situation where a woman would phone round her friends, declaring, "I'm organising a baby shower for my sister, the human incubator." Pregnant women do not lose their personhood as soon as conception occurs in their fallopian tubes, as the human incubator analogy implies.

For the pro-life feminist, it is not enough to recognise and question the egotism of a position which exalts the self at all costs. We need to make it clear that we respect the right of women and men to bodily integrity and the right to give or withhold free consent; we need to go further and ensure that the importance of bodily integrity is not left out of the abortion debate by the pro-life side in the same way that the right to life is ignored by abortion advocates. Anyone who has ever had the misfortune to be coerced, threatened, emotionally blackmailed or physically forced to submit to any unwanted intervention will know what a terrifying and humiliating abuse that is—and whereas both men and women need protection from unwanted intrusion, medical or otherwise, I would argue that women are more likely than men to be vulnerable to such interference. There are therefore very few situations in which it can be regarded as ethical to treat a person by force, even if their lives are in serious danger (such as in the case of the hunger striker). A doctor must surely be able to prove that the person concerned lacks capacity to the extent of being incapable of giving or withholding consent.

Acknowledging and protecting the right to life of the unborn child does not ignore or cancel out the right to bodily integrity. However, there will always be situations when the rights of one person may appear to be in conflict with the rights of another, and under these limited circumstances, the more significant right—in the case of abortion, the right to life—must be paramount. If abortion were a lifesaving, life-affirming procedure that did not involve any other human life, pro-life feminists would be standing shoulder-to-shoulder with radical feminists outside abortion facilities in solidarity with the abortion providers. But abortion does involve another human life; every medical and technological advance grants more and more authority to this position, and even abortion's most vociferous supporters struggle to dismiss this any longer.

A second point that is not made strongly enough concerns what abortion actually involves. One of the most dishonest and disingenuous lines shouted at pro-lifers during counter-demonstrations is "Get out of my uterus!" Abortion pretty much by definition involves a third party getting into a woman's uterus—directly through surgical means or indirectly through chemical interference—and the unborn child would be a great deal safer if certain people really did keep out of the uterus. Women in general do not perform their own abortions, and even chemical abortion has to be prescribed by a medical professional. The debate surrounding life issues such as abortion tends to be focused entirely upon the feelings and beliefs of the individual—my life, my sovereignty over my body, my autonomy, my healthcare choices, my rights, my belief systems—and forgets that these actions involve a third party whose job it is to operate the vacuum aspirator, to insert the needle, to sign off the prescription, to clean up the mess and whose choice to refuse is not always legally protected. There is an underlying belief that the medical profession is under an obligation to involve itself in abortion, but if autonomy and conscience are as important as abortion campaigners claim to believe, then what about the autonomy of medical professionals who say no? What right does society have to bully, coax and blackmail others into carrying the burden of ending human life? Doctors and midwives who refuse to be involved in abortion as a matter of conscience face discrimination in the workplace, are portrayed as heartless and unprofessional in pro-abortion literature and in some cases have to fight for their jobs in court.

Even if there are a steady stream of doctors who are prepared to put themselves forward, the question still needs to be asked, should anyone, particularly a person who has been trained to preserve life, be placed in such a position? In the end, killing a human being under any circumstances is never an easy act to commit even if an individual is convinced that it is justified, such as in the case of self-defence. Killing involves crossing a boundary that human beings are hard-wired never to cross. According to Captain Robert Cardona, a psychiatrist specialising in combat stress: "Killing unleashes emotions few people are prepared to deal with."[3] Even soldiers, who are trained to kill and enter a profession they know is likely to involve having to kill, struggle to deal with the consequences. Post-traumatic stress disorder is a major effect of serving in a theatre of war.

Likewise, state executioners struggle to deal with the harsh reality of ending the lives of condemned prisoners. A former executioner from the state of Texas spoke about these experiences and commented: "Taking a life is not a pleasant thing to do. You have a condemned [inmate] that didn't do anything to you.... If you let the judge be the executioner, I think he would give a second thought about sending somebody to be executed."[4]

It could hardly be deemed unreasonable, therefore, if members of the medical profession, who are positively not trained to end life, struggle with the emotional and psychological effects of performing abortions, and studies going back forty years have drawn attention to this phenomenon. According to one early study of abortionists: "obsessional thinking about abortion, depression, fatigue, anger, lowered self-esteem, and identity conflicts were prominent. The symptom complex was considered a 'transient reactive disorder', similar to 'combat fatigue'."[5]

Unlike activists, who can hide behind their own eloquent rhetoric and speak of tissue and cells, of termination, interruption, procedures, autonomy, choice and reproductive rights, those who perform the abortions face the ugly, undisguised nature of abortion every day of their

[3] Charles Duhigg, "Enemy Contact. Kill 'em, Kill 'em", *Los Angeles Times*, 18 July 2004, http://articles.latimes.com/2004/jul/18/world/fg-killing18/2.

[4] "Secondary Trauma of Executions", Montana Abolition Coalition, 2017, http://mtabolitionco.org/issues/secondary-trauma/.

[5] Quoted in Rachel McNair, *Achieving Peace in the Abortion War* (New York: iUniverse, 2008), p. 9.

working lives. As Dr Anthony Levatino, an American former abortionist, has said: "I want the general public to know that the doctors know that this is a person; this is a baby. That this is not some kind of blob of tissue."[6]

The effects on those performing abortions has been well documented by experts such as Dr Philip Ney and organisations for former abortionists, including And Then There Were None and Society of Centurions. Former abortionists such as Dr Bernard Nathanson have spoken candidly about the impact performing abortions had on their personal lives, and there are hundreds if not thousands of testimonies in the public domain from doctors, nurses and others involved in abortion who resigned because they were no longer able to deal with the horror of what they were doing.

The effects of involvement in abortion can touch even those who are not direct participants. A couple once discussed with me the crisis of conscience they had faced together when the husband, J., innocently took up an administrative position at a hospital in the Obs and Gynae department, only to find himself processing abortion forms. J.'s only part in the procedure was to process those forms, but he saw them as death warrants and likened himself to a concentration camp guard. After being told he had no choice but to continue with his work, he was subjected to taunting and bullying from colleagues and eventually resigned. He never witnessed an abortion, still less did he perform one, but his sense of being a cog in the abortion machine drove him to despair.

Perhaps the saddest example of a doctor broken by abortion was the case of Dr Charles Rickards, one of Britain's

[6] Quoted in Randy Alcorn, *Pro-Life Answers to Pro-Choice Questions* (Danvers, Mass.: Multnomah Books, Crown Publishing Group, 2009), p. 206.

leading gynaecologists when Parliament passed the 1967 Abortion Act. In 1971, his local newspaper reported that he "walked into a stormy sea, his wrists bound with shoe-laces after months in despair of a world where unborn babies could be legally destroyed." Another gynaecologist and colleague of Dr Rickards said of him: "He wanted to save life. Destroying it was something he could never face. He and older gynaecologists like myself believe abortion is inherently evil."[7]

The right to conscientious objection from abortion is enshrined in English law, but with the law being interpreted ever more narrowly and doctors who exercise their rights being demonised as antiwoman, the right of a doctor to professional integrity is increasingly at risk.

---

[7] *A Way of Life* (UK: Society for the Protection of Unborn Children [SPUC], 2002), p. 97.

Pregnancy: Problems and Perspective

Truthfully, being pregnant is changing me as a person. Each day is part of this amazing journey that has completely shifted the focus of my life and made me re-evaluate my personal and professional goals.

—Holly Madison

The determination of radical feminists to pathologise pregnancy and turn it into an ideological battleground should not distract pro-life feminists from acknowledging the harsh reality of pregnancy as experienced by a sizeable minority of women. To a limited extent, every pregnancy is a "crisis pregnancy" because it involves embarking upon a life-changing journey into the unknown which will inevitably involve many moments of joy and happiness but also the moments of fear, stress and grief any mother can expect to experience at some point in the mother-child relationship.

However, the word "crisis" is not of itself a declaration of a state of emergency. The word was originally a medical term referring to the turning point of an illness in the direction of either recovery or death. The etymological root of the word is the Greek *krisis* meaning "decision" not disaster. More generally, the word "crisis" in the English language has referred for hundreds of years to a decisive moment or the making of a decision.

Interestingly, in Chinese, the two characters that make up the word for crisis represent danger and opportunity, suggesting that a moment of crisis may have a disastrous consequence but also offers the possibility of a positive result. In the literal sense of the word, crisis will always be an apt way to describe even the happiest and most expected of pregnancies.

However, there is no avoiding the fact that for some women, pregnancy is a lonely, difficult and indeed at times distressing experience. As I have learnt to my own cost, there are few lonelier places than a sick bed, battling chronic hyperemesis whilst well-meaning individuals insinuate that this is all really a fuss about nothing and a few dry crackers would sort out the morning sickness in no time. When a woman is physically incapacitated, it has a knock-on effect on her mental health, emotional well-being and relationships. More importantly, we should acknowledge the obvious point that pregnancy is a life-changing experience, however it progresses and however it ends.

Women Alone

One of the most distressing and misunderstood complications of pregnancy is hyperemesis gravidarum (HG), a rare form of pregnancy illness which causes persistent nausea and vomiting as well as other rarer symptoms such as photophobia and hypersensitivity to noise and movement. HG appeared in the media spotlight briefly when the Duchess of Cambridge experienced it while pregnant with the heir to the English throne, but even then, her condition was dismissed by some as "what you call morning sickness if you are a princess."

Some 15 percent of HG pregnancies in the United States end in abortion.[1] The overwhelming majority of these abortions are unwanted, causing high levels of grief, guilt and anger from women who are driven to abortion as a result of being unable to cope with their symptoms. A report by Pregnancy Sickness Support[2] in cooperation with British abortion provider BPAS described the level of unwanted abortion among desperate women as "unacceptable", though the abortion provider's indignation is hard to take entirely seriously here. If an organisation such as BPAS claims to support women's choices, it is hard to see why they are blithely carrying out unwanted abortions on women rather than drawing their attention to the alternatives and discussing HG treatment options with them.

The treatment of women with HG by medical professionals in general makes for depressing reading, with women complaining that they were patronised, dismissed, instructed to pull themselves together or advised that it was "all in the mind"[3] (my own doctor crossly instructed me to nibble dry crackers when I told her I was vomiting blood and treated me to a lecture about how silly I was to "purposefully" dehydrate myself). It is particularly concerning that doctors who have the power to sign abortion

[1] Joan Christodoulou-Smith et al., "Posttraumatic Stress Symptoms following Pregnancy Complicated by Hyperemesis Gravidarum", *Journal of Maternal-Fetal and Neonatal Medicine* (2011): 1, http://www.helpher.org/downloads/Posttraumatic%20stress%20symptoms%20following%20pregnancy%20complicated%20by%20hyperemesis%20gravidarum.pdf.

[2] "I Could Not Survive Another Day", Pregnancy Sickness Support, accessed 12 February 2017, https://www.pregnancysicknesssupport.org.uk/documents/resources/Termination_A4_indd.pdf.

[3] Margaret O'Hara, "Women's Experience of Hyperemesis Gravidarum: Results of Self- Reported Online Surveys", Pregnancy Sickness Support, 2013, https://www.pregnancysicknesssupport.org.uk/documents/HCPconference slides/womens-experience-2013-MOH.pdf.

referral forms should be so woefully ignorant of the available treatments for HG or even the existence of the illness itself. It is little wonder that women with HG—deprived of treatment, support or even courtesy from their doctors and midwives—should be driven to undergo abortion, but it is laughable to claim that, in doing so, the medical profession are assisting their freedom of choice.

Women in Danger

According to Britain's National Health Service, 30 percent of domestic abuse begins during pregnancy, whilst preexisting abuse tends to worsen when a woman is pregnant.[4] Violence increases the risk of miscarriage, premature delivery and stillbirth, with domestic violence accounting for some 12 percent of maternal deaths in Britain a decade ago.[5] A significant minority of women experience domestic violence during their lives whether or not they also experience pregnancy, but pregnancy renders a woman vulnerable physically, emotionally and mentally, making abuse harder to avoid or escape.

The refusal of a woman to abort a baby has been cited in a number of high-profile court cases, such as the case of London woman Malorie Bantala,[6] who was beaten by her ex-boyfriend and an accomplice with the deliberate intention of killing her unborn son when she refused to

[4] "Domestic Abuse", NHS, accessed 12 February 2017, http://www.nhs .uk/conditions/pregnancy-and-baby/pages/domestic-abuse-pregnant.aspx.

[5] "What Is Domestic Violence?", Baby Centre, last reviewed May 2013, http://www.babycentre.co.uk/a563127/domestic-violence.

[6] Ashitha Nagesh, "Man Jailed for Life after Beating Heavily Pregnant Ex to Kill Her Unborn Baby", Metro, 11 February 2016, http://metro.co.uk /2016/02/11/man-jailed-for-life-after-beating-heavily-pregnant-ex-to-kill -her-unborn-baby-5676795/.

abort him. This case mirrors a similar crime in New York in which a man was sentenced to over thirty years' imprisonment for attacking his ex-girlfriend Mia Jones, inflicting life-threatening injuries and killing her unborn child. These two cases represent an extreme form of domestic violence against pregnant women, and the judge in the Mia Jones case stated during his closing remarks: "In the over 20 years that I have been involved in criminal law, I have never seen such callous and inhumane acts towards a person one was intimate with for so long."[7] However, all violence towards an unarmed and defenceless person can be characterised as callous and inhumane; in general, any act of violence against a pregnant woman will carry with it a cruel indifference to the fate of two innocent lives.

Abortion does not offer a way out of abuse for a pregnant woman and gives violence the final victory, but to ignore the needs of women in such situations is neither pro-woman nor pro-life.

Resetting the Emotional Compass

Campaigning organisations of all persuasions tend to focus a great deal of attention on the most extreme situations, and a disproportionate amount of time and energy is spent by both pro-abortion and antiabortion groups arguing over the hard cases. The hard cases obviously need to be carefully considered, but a danger with overemphasising the distressing extreme is the avoidance of real interaction with the experiences of the majority of pregnant

---

[7] Emily Saul, "'Monster' Who Beat Pregnant Girlfriend Gets Maximum Sentence", *New York Post*, 1 March 2016, http://nypost.com/2016/03/01 /monster-who-beat-pregnant-girlfriend-gets-maximum-sentence/.

women and a gradual distorting of the public understanding of both pregnancy and the major reasons why women have abortions.

For all the intense emotion that surrounds it, pregnancy is neither a terminal illness nor a form of enslavement for which abortion is the cure. Whilst acknowledging the difficulties faced by some women during pregnancy, we have to challenge the inflated emotional rhetoric that surrounds the abortion debate, typified by statements such as "The ultimate assault on a woman's body [is] requiring her to carry a child she has decided she cannot have." It is hard not to cheer, reading Live Action's Kristi Burton Brown's response:

> Really? *Really?* The ultimate assault on my body is carrying a child? That's worse than murdering me, torturing me, raping me, sacrificing me to a false god, using me as a sex slave, or cannabalizing me (all things that still happen to women in this world, by the way).[8]

It is in the nature of shock-jock journalism to make provocative statements, but it is hard to believe that any abortion campaigner seriously believes that a pro-life doctor is some kind of misogynist master criminal, committing worse crimes against women's dignity than traffickers, torturers or murderers. Laughable as such exaggerated statements may appear, the obsession with abortion and the tendency to cast women as the hapless victims of their own children trivialises the real exploitation and suffering of women that continues around the world in all countries and cultures.

---

[8] Kristi Burton Brown, "Is There Such a Thing as a Pro-Life Feminist?", *Live Action Blog*, 23 January 2012, http://liveaction.org/blog/is-there-such-a -thing-as-a-pro-life-feminist/.

On a more fundamental level, treating pregnancy as though it were an unavoidable life-altering injury insults women in much the same way some feminists accuse men of doing when they attempt chivalry. It assumes that women are so delicate and so helpless that they need rescuing from their own physiological state, that women cannot be expected to tolerate nine months of pregnancy in order to ensure the survival of a temporarily dependent human being.

Ironically, the tendency to cast pregnancy as a condition a woman can contract through no agency of her own, much the way a person might catch flu or a bout of shingles, assumes a woman's inability to take responsibility for her own actions and relegates her to the position of a minor or a mentally incapacitated person. Yes, it takes two to tango as the old saying goes, and the father of the child is equally responsible for its existence; yes, it is certainly true that it remains far too easy for men to wriggle out of their own responsibilities, leaving the mother to cope alone, and society has yet fully to address this problem. Yes, as has already been noted, a very small percentage of all pregnancies are conceived through rape. However, the inconvenient truth must also be confronted that the majority of conceptions occur as a result of the actions of two consenting adults. In spite of the many attempts to thwart its inherent purpose, sexual intercourse remains a procreative act, whether or not the couple concerned wish it to be (I personally eat for pleasure and rather resent the fact that eating chocolate causes me to put on weight. I can rail against the injustice of it as much as I like, but nature cannot hear my protestations that eating should be purely recreational and consequence free). Heterosexual sex is the kind of activity that can lead to pregnancy. It is fairly pointless for loud-mouthed individuals to tell women that they exercised their right to choose when they dropped their knickers, but a more appropriate response might be to remember that freedom—fought for and defended at so many points in human history—is a delicate commodity which must always be handled responsibly and selflessly. True freedom is not synonymous with lawlessness or anarchy; it presupposes but does not endorse the ability to make a bad choice, whilst a necessary part of the adult exercise of freedom is a willingness to deal compassionately with its many consequences. Society should act compassionately by offering pregnant women and their children—both unborn and born—as much help and support as necessary for them to flourish, but a couple should also be expected to act compassionately and nurture the child they have created, who did not ask to be conceived and should not be punished with death for existing.

A Path Worth Walking:
The Changing Nature of the Debate

Over the past twenty years, there has been an audible increase in strong female voices prepared to make the case for a new approach to the abortion debate which embraces both the rights of women and the rights of the unborn. Pro-life feminist groups are changing the tone of the debate and offering a platform to women who oppose abortion and other attacks on life, but are not prepared to resign from the struggle for full emancipation either.

There is a great need for this after decades of intellectual stalemate. Pro-life feminism offers a vision that is both wholly on the side of women and wholly on the side of science, which seeks just, nonviolent answers to the problems facing pregnant women in difficulty. Pro-life campaigning is as much a part of social justice as campaigning to provide vaccination programmes for infants in sub-Saharan Africa, because the first of all human rights is the right to life. It is the fatally disastrous blind spot in current human rights campaigning, the failure to acknowledge the rights of every member of the human family, but pro-life feminism represents a human rights movement which excludes no human life under any circumstances.

Groups such as Feminists for Life of America have made a valuable contribution to the debate by reminding both feminists and pro-life campaigners that the early feminists had a very different view of the unborn child and saw abortion for what it was—not a tool of empowerment but evidence that a patriarchal society was failing women. Feminist pioneer Elizabeth Cady Stanton lamented over a hundred years ago: "When we consider that women are treated as property, it is degrading to women that we should treat our children as property to be disposed of as we see fit." It raises the question that women today may continue to be encouraged to treat their children as property because society has not yet let go of the notion that women are themselves property, or at best the lesser man, victims of their own inferior biology who can only be liberated through a primeval act of child sacrifice.

Pro-life feminists not only seek to reclaim their feminist birthright from mainstream feminists who demand absolute submission to the doctrine of abortion on demand. In order to address the continued injustices facing women and their unborn children, it is necessary to return to the early days of feminism and the world in which feminism first emerged. It is easy in the twenty-first century to be complacent about the independence women enjoy on a day-to-day basis. Every single day of my life I enjoy freedoms that were denied women not so very far in the past—I can put my debit card into an ATM and withdraw money from my bank account because I am entitled to financial independence; the money in my bank account is there courtesy of the work I am entitled to perform, thanks to the university degree I was able to achieve. Every five years, I go to a polling station near my home and put an "x" in a box, indicating which parliamentary candidate I wish to represent me. The chances are that I will forget, as I do so, the women who campaigned, who were imprisoned, force-fed and in some cases died for my right to vote or, indeed, the millions of men who died for my continued right to do so.

The overwhelming majority of people today, I suspect, are appalled by the thought that women did not achieve anything close to full emancipation in the West until the mid-twentieth century and that women for so many centuries have been denied the freedoms and opportunities that their male counterparts have been granted. Feminism did not appear out of nowhere with the single intention of disenfranchising men, but unlike the inward-looking, self-obsessed vision of womanhood presented by some strands of contemporary feminism, the early feminists promoted the rights of women because they believed the strength and health of society to be intimately bound up with the status of women.

Mary Wollstonecraft's contribution to feminist philosophy is a matter of some debate. She has been described as the founder of modern feminist philosophy, but a body of opinion questions whether she may be described as a feminist at all, largely, perhaps, because contemporary feminism has travelled so far from the convictions held by Wollstonecraft. Her ground-breaking work, *A Vindication of the Rights of Woman,*[9] advocates a position few would regard as controversial, seeking to strengthen not destroy the family unit. She condemns the tyrannical and insulting attitude of her age that weakness, vanity and stupidity were somehow "natural" to womankind when society itself was cynically and despotically encouraging girls to develop into "the toy of man, his rattle",[10] possessed of "spaniel-like affection"[11] and "tainted by coquettish arts".[12]

Whereas I would find some of Wollstonecraft's observations about marriage as problematic as her narrow focus on the experience of the middle-class woman (a criticism I would not limit to Wollstonecraft), it is important to note the extent to which *Vindication* supports and seeks to strengthen marriage, on the grounds that a strong and reasonable woman makes a better wife and mother, particularly as a mother is the primary educator of the next generation. As she puts it: "The woman who strengthens her body and exercises her mind will, by managing her family and practising various virtues, become the friend, and not the humble dependent of her husband."[13] She also draws attention to the vulnerability and humiliation faced by women such as young widows, when they were deprived of their male protector and society had robbed them of any possibility of independence. Wollstonecraft was by no means the only person to criticise the oppression of women. She quotes a certain Dr Day, who, in one of his books about the progressive education he had given his daughter, stated:

[9] Mary Wollstonecraft, *A Vindication of the Rights of Woman* (Mineola, N.Y.: Dover Publications, 1996).
[10] Ibid., p. 33.
[11] Ibid.
[12] Ibid., p. 30.
[13] Ibid., p. 28.

If women are in general feeble in body and mind, it arises less from nature than from education. We encourage a vicious indolence and inactivity, which we falsely call delicacy, instead of hardening their minds by the severer principles of reason and philosophy, we breed them to useless arts, which terminate in vanity and sensuality. In most of the countries which I had visited, they are taught nothing of an higher nature than a few modulations of the voice, or useless postures of the body; their time is consumed in sloth or trifles, and trifles become the only pursuits capable of interesting them. *We seem to forget, that it is upon the qualities of the female sex that our own domestic comforts and the education of our children must depend. And what are the comforts or the education which a race of beings, corrupted from their infancy, and unacquainted with all the duties of life, are fitted to bestow?* To touch a musical instrument with useless skill, to dissipate their husband's patrimony in riotous and unnecessary expenses, these are the only arts cultivated by women in most of the polished nations I had seen. And the consequences are uniformly such as may be expected to proceed from such polluted sources, private misery and public servitude.[14]

The ability of a woman to cultivate her own mind was not simply a matter of justice for women, a matter of her right to education on a par with men; it was recognised as having serious implications for the moral well-being of society. Any movement which seeks to improve the status and protection of a given group, whether it is women, children or minorities, should do so for the sake of humanity not simply for the good of that section of society, because in the end we are all part of the human family. When pro-abortion protestors disrupt public meetings screaming, "Women's rights are human rights!" I agree with them

[14] Ibid., p. 40; emphasis added.

entirely—I simply wish they would find more adult ways of articulating the obvious.

It is therefore by returning to the vision of the early feminists that the foundations of a new woman's movement are being laid, a movement in which feminists can dare to stand against the status quo as campaigners for centuries have done, even if this time, women must sometimes stand against other women. Blogger Julia Herrington, in the story of her change of heart on abortion, wrote: "In every other facet of feminism, we celebrate a woman's body; we honor her identity as a female. Abortion requires the silencing of a woman's body and the unmitigated dismissing of her gender."[15] The intellectual journey of pro-life feminist surely begins with the question "Can't we do better than this?" and furthermore, "Don't women deserve better than this?"

That women have been exploited throughout history is an uncomfortable fact—that women continue to get a raw deal in many parts of the world including our own is even more so. Glib dismissals will not do, nor will the efforts by some men to demonise women on account of a movement that may not represent them. When feminism first embraced abortion as a right, a key principle of human rights campaigning was forgotten—namely, that in participating in a just campaign to liberate women, it is never acceptable to support a system which subjugates others.

If the pro-life battle is to be won, it will be won by women with men standing shoulder-to-shoulder with us, not presuming to lead us, not speaking on our behalf, but standing in solidarity with us. The battle to protect and

[15] Julia Herrington, "How I Changed My Mind about Abortion", Christ and Pop Culture, accessed 12 February 2017, http://www.patheos.com/blogs/christandpopculture/how-i-changed-my-mind-about-abortion/.

respect human life at its most vulnerable is the great social justice campaign of our day, and there is no better movement to fight it than a pro-life feminist movement which embraces and celebrates the dignity of women, the sanctity of life and the need for men and women to work together with complementary gifts, yet as equals in pursuit of the common good. As David Albert Jones warns in his book *The Soul of the Embryo*, "The path of the pro-life feminist is currently a very hard and lonely road indeed."[16] There is no denying that this is the case, but I would perhaps respond by quoting an old proverb I was taught as a teenager: "Fear not the path of truth for the lack of people walking it." And I do believe that this path is worth walking.

---

[16] David Albert Jones, *The Soul of the Embryo* (London, UK: Continuum, 2004), p. 205.

APPENDIX 1

About Abortion: Another One-Sided Look at Abortion in America[*]

Desperation to avoid talking to women about the reality of abortion and its alternatives exposes the hypocrisy behind the rhetoric of choice, repeated and reinforced throughout the recent book by Carol Sanger, About Abortion: Terminating Pregnancy in Twenty-First-Century America.[†]

The first comment I should make before launching into a review of Carol Sanger's book *About Abortion: Terminating Pregnancy in Twenty-First-Century America* is that she is no Ann Furedi.[1] As the name of the publisher (Harvard University Press) suggests, Carol Sanger is an academic, a law

[*] The following originally appeared in Fiorella Nash, "'About Abortion': Another One-Sided Look at Abortion in America", *Catholic World Report*, 8 August 2017, www.catholicworldreport.com/2017/08/08/about-abortion-another-one-sided-look-at-abortion-in-america/.

[†] Carol Sanger, *About Abortion: Terminating Pregnancy in Twenty-First-Century America* (Cambridge, Mass.: Harvard University Press, 2017).

[1] Ann Furedi is a prominent UK abortion provider and apologist who authored the book *The Moral Case for Abortion* (London: Palgrave Macmillan, 2016). For my review of her book, see the following appendix as well as Fiorella Nash, "A Moral Case for Abortion?", *Catholic World Report*, 18 November 2016, www.catholicworldreport.com/2016/11/18/a-moral-case-for-abortion/.

professor at Columbia, and she writes intelligently and skillfully about her area of expertise. However, the book begins with what is either a naughty fib or yet another example of how deluded abortion activists are in terms of the way they see themselves. We are informed early on that "this book is neither for abortion nor against it."[2] I have never kept a tally of how many abortion-related books I have read over the years, but the one thing I can say with certainty is that there is no such thing as a neutral book on abortion, and Sanger's book is no such thing. The mask of neutrality slips almost immediately. Quite rightly, Sanger criticizes "uncivil and fractious exchange" (p. xiv) on abortion, but only refers to a pro-life congressman "who shouted 'baby-killer' on the floor of the House in 2010" (ibid.). In the interests of balance, she might also have referred to abortion campaigners who dress up as giant vaginas and scream obscenities at children on marches, spit in the faces of priests and taunt pro-lifers as they pray. She informs us that "abortion is, in the first instance, a medical procedure" (p. 4). Yes, if by that we mean simply that doctors perform them using drugs or surgical instruments and they generally take place in a clinical setting; but if abortion were simply a medical procedure akin, for example, to the removal of a rumbling appendix, it would never have become the subject of such passionate debate in the first place. Throughout the book, there is an underlying assumption that Sanger's readers will all agree with her and are naturally pro-choice. Therefore, parental consent laws "excite our sense of injustice" and "rightfully rile us up" (p. 157). Us? *Our* sense? Speak for yourself, Carol.

---

[2] Sanger, *About Abortion*, p. xiv. Subsequent quotations from this work will be cited in the text.

Whereas Sanger shows a detailed knowledge of law, her understanding of the dynamics of the pro-life movement is woefully inadequate. "For many people, abortion is about religion" (p. 7). No one is going to deny that faith plays a significant part in mobilizing resistance to abortion, but Sanger appears unaware of the existence of secular pro-life organizations such as Secular Pro-Life, Feminists for Life of America and UK-based groups such as the Society for the Protection of Unborn Children, which was founded as a secular, nonpartisan organization to oppose the legalization of abortion in Britain. Sanger informs readers that "we do not yet know Pope Francis' position, if any, on Catholic candidates or voters with regard to abortion beliefs or practices. His statements about abortion so far have been that the Church might lessen its obsession with the topic" (p. 8). Is this the same pope who has spoken repeatedly of the innocent victims of abortion who are "condemned unjustly"[3] and has described abortion as "a tragedy"?[4] Would this be the Pope Francis who has stated, "It is not 'progressive' to try to resolve problems by eliminating a human life"?[5]

No book about abortion is complete without the author making shallow attempts at undermining religious beliefs

[3] Address of Holy Father Francis to Participants in the Meeting Organized by the International Federation of Catholic Medical Associations, 20 September 2013, https://w2.vatican.va/content/francesco/en/speeches/2013/september /documents/papa-francesco_20130920_associazioni-medici-cattolici.html.

[4] Letter of His Holiness Pope Francis according to Which an Indulgence Is Granted to the Faithful on the Occasion of the Extraordinary Jubilee of Mercy, 1 September 2015, https://w2.vatican.va/content/francesco/en/letters /2015/documents/papa-francesco_20150901_lettera-indulgenza-giubileo -misericordia.html.

[5] Francis, apostolic exhortation *Evangelii gaudium* (Joy of the Gospel), 24 November 2013, no. 214, http://www.vatican.va/evangelii-gaudium/en/files /assets/basic-html/page166.html.

by explaining them away as pseudo-political constructs; and Sanger clearly could not help herself when trying to explain the point of the Gospel account of the Visitation (Luke 1:39–56). I was intrigued to be told that John the Baptist leaping in the womb (v. 41) was all a ploy to settle a power struggle between the followers of John the Baptist and the followers of Jesus; indeed, any reference to the unborn in spiritual writings appears to have been "a piece of a spiritual political project of the time" (p. 76). It is a pity Sanger did not take the trouble to explore what Jews and Christians actually believe rather than indulging in her own half-baked interpretations; but it does not appear to occur to her that unborn life may only have become a focus of political machinations as a result of the battle over legal abortion. For centuries, a description of an unborn baby leaping in the womb at the sound of a woman's voice would not have required hastily explaining away. Almost on cue, we are also treated to the much-repeated claim that Catholic doctrine on abortion has changed because that clever chap Aquinas thought ensoulment happened forty or ninety days after conception. Is Sanger really unaware that, despite centuries of controversy about ensoulment, abortion was always seen as seriously wrong?

Sanger's understanding of history is similarly lacking in context. She talks about the use of preserved fetuses as part of fairground sideshows, stating that "these displays were not regarded as disrespectful or sacrilegious as they might be today" (p. 79). The implication is that societies past did not afford the same respect to the unborn. These were, of course, the same societies who displayed "freaks" in sideshows and failed to treat bearded ladies, children with deformed limbs and conjoined twins as persons deserving of dignity. By the same logic, we should stop treating people with disabilities with respect because people in the past

did not always do so. It is hard to see what point Sanger
seems to be trying to prove here other than to demonstrate
that morbid curiosity has a long history.

Sanger shows a similarly poor understanding of the
socio-political situation outside the United States. I actually laughed reading her solemn pronouncement that "in
contrast to other places—all of Western Europe, say—
where teenage sexuality is accepted as developmentally
normal, in the United States it is still taken as a sign of
trouble, particularly for girls" (pp. 10–11). Really? It
always strikes me as odd that the very people who are
so keen to draw attention to the apparent inconsistency
between Church teaching and the views of Catholics "on
the ground" nevertheless assume that the pronouncements of out-of-touch sexual health agencies are entirely
representative of what parents believe or want for their
children. Britain is certainly a more aggressively secular
country than the United States, but I have yet to meet
many parents in leafy Surrey who think it a jolly good
idea for their little Siennas and Sebastians to start copulat-
ing behind the bike shed after school.

Never Grasping the Nettle

A major flaw in Sanger's analysis, as with so many books
defending abortion, is an unwillingness to admit to the
very basic, very straightforward reason people oppose
abortion—it ends a human life. That is the reason people dedicate years of their lives to campaigning against
abortion; that is the reason people pray outside abortion
facilities; that is the reason people sacrifice their careers
and endure financial hardship and public ridicule; that is
the reason pro-life people find abortion so abhorrent that

they feel compelled to fight it at every turn. If abortion were merely a medical procedure like any other, I would not have devoted so much of my own time and energy to fighting it. I would go further and say that I would probably be standing outside abortion facilities protesting in defense of keeping them open.

Instead of acknowledging the obvious, Sanger proposes: "For those who feel anxious about the stability of this once reliable boy-girl scheme, abortion can be deeply unsettling. It frees women to act more like men" (p. 15). She then cites a pro-abortion legal judgement to justify this position. More chilling is her analysis of female authority in terms of "control over whether and what kind of new persons will come into being—the gatekeeping of human existence" (p. 16). Apparently, "the radical character of this primal gatekeeping may disturb those not used to thinking in terms of women's superior authority" (ibid.). That's one way of looking at it. Another might be to consider the more serious question of whether a human being— female or male—should have the power of life or death over another, and what the implications are for a society of exalting any section of the population to the role of "gatekeeper" in the first place. Naturally, it disturbs those of us who have no desire to "get used" to the idea of adults as agents of extermination.

A work that is supposed to be "neither for or against" makes no real attempt to engage with the genuine reasons why pro-life campaigners exist at all. Every pro-life argument is a manipulative tactic: "Casting women as killers not simply of vulnerable foetuses but of vulnerable minority foetuses is a clever move" (p. 34). Not really, no. Women do not need to be "cast" in a role they freely choose; another awkward aspect of "choice" is that it involves accepting moral responsibility for the act chosen.

As the book admits, albeit grudgingly at different points, abortion involves killing a fetus; therefore, a person having an abortion is a killer of a fetus. This is a fact, not an act of political posturing. The fact that abortions are performed because a baby has a disability or is female ought to be a cause of disquiet among abortion advocates, but that would involve soul-searching, and that was never the purpose of this book.

An Unwelcome Window into the Womb

The message that resonates throughout the book should hearten pro-life campaigners everywhere: abortion advocates really, *really* hate ultrasound images. The opportunity— through modern technology—to be seen allows the unborn to mount a defense of their own, simply by being visible; and this is not going down at all well with the promoters of abortion. Sanger dedicates a vast section of the book to arguing against state legislation requiring women to view an ultrasound and employs all her rhetorical ability to undermining the value of ultrasound imagery altogether. "The requirement confuses wanted with unwanted pregnancies, as antiabortion legislators seem happy to do" (p. xi), or just draws attention to the fact that—for all her many attempts at pretending that the fetus is some kind of social construct— a baby will never obligingly become a blob because it is unwanted.

Laws making the viewing of ultrasounds mandatory (or at least offering to show the woman the ultrasound, as some state laws demand) are acts of punishment, as far as Sanger is concerned, because they are unnecessary. "Women— even young women—understand very well what an abortion is," she writes. "They understand that abortion ends pregnancy and that if they have an abortion, they will not have a baby: that is its very point" (p. 23). Yes, except that there is a difference between knowing that you are ending the physiological state of pregnancy and knowing that you are ending a life; and abortion promotors go to considerable lengths to avoid that thorny subject. Margaret Cuthill, co-founder of British Victims of Abortion (now ARCH—Abortion Recovery Care and Helpline[6]), speaks candidly about her two abortions and the repeated assurances she received that it was "nothing" and "just cells", only to undergo an ultrasound scan to work out why she still felt pregnant following her abortion. She saw the grainy image of a tiny baby—a surviving twin—and realized the full horror of what her two abortions had involved. Yes, Margaret had known the pregnancy would end, but by her own admission, she would never have gone ahead with the abortion if she had had the scan beforehand, and she could not face another abortion when she could clearly see her baby.

The desperation to avoid talking to women, not just about the reality of abortion, but even the alternatives, exposes the hypocrisy behind the rhetoric of choice; but this hypocrisy is merely repeated and reinforced throughout the book. Sanger approvingly quotes a Supreme Court judgement against the provision of information about the risks associated with abortion on the grounds that "the Commonwealth does not, and surely would not, compel similar disclosure of every possible peril of necessary surgery or of simple vaccination" (p. 30). Leaving aside the fact that abortion is not "necessary surgery" or anything akin to a "simple vaccination", the statement is patently false. An uninformed choice is hardly empowering insofar

---

[6] See their website at http://www.archtrust.org.uk/.

as it constitutes a choice at all—we value your choice, sisters, but we're not going to tell you anything about the implications or risks of your choice, and we are certainly not going to suggest that there are alternatives which would make your choice an actual *choice*. In other areas of medicine, patients are obliged to hear all sorts of information they might rather not know: I am not sure my father was absolutely thrilled to be informed by his doctor that open heart surgery would involve his ribs being broken; I did not particularly appreciate the ominous warning before eye surgery that there was a risk—albeit tiny—of permanent sight loss. But that information is given out for a reason. If a patient is to sign his name on a consent form, that consent must be given freely and in reasonable knowledge of the potential consequences—all of them, not just the ones a clinic feels like talking about.

The determination of abortion advocates to prevent women from receiving full information about abortion and, indeed, about the gestational development of their own offspring is a major contradiction in feminist thinking that simply cannot continue to be ignored. Sanger, like many abortion apologists, expresses extreme hostility to mandatory ultrasounds for abortion-minded women, but it is in the act of dismissing these laws as "unsavory" and "pernicious" that the moral confusion of the pro-abortion position is most in evidence. Comparing such laws with a court case involving a woman who witnessed her little boy being hit and killed by a car, Sanger informs us that viewing an ultrasound image of a baby prior to abortion is being, "in effect, asked by law to witness her child soon before its death" and to acknowledge "the reality of its impending death" (pp. 108, 118). Sanger dedicates pages of verbal and intellectual gymnastics to turning the viewing of an unborn baby into a massive pro-life conspiracy, whilst ignoring the central points raised by such legislation. First, if it is so distressing for a woman to see her child immediately before it is killed, surely this raises the rather larger question as to whether it is morally acceptable to kill the baby at all. Second, if women are to be treated as fully emancipated, empowered adults, it is hardly unreasonable to ask women to face the full consequences of their actions. Short of turning the planet into one vast safe space replete with Playdoh and films of gamboling ponies, it is difficult to see how or—more pertinently—why women should be protected from the reality of their own choices in the name of empowerment.

The now-routine use of ultrasound was, according to Sanger, "not a bad deal for pro-life advocates" (p. 80), though she might just as easily have said that it was a pretty good deal for both women and the unborn. Where Sanger has a point about the invasion of privacy is in the rare instances in which there is a legal requirement for a vaginal transducer to be used rather than an abdominal wand (this involves the insertion of a probe into the woman's vagina rather than being drawn across her abdomen). This would seem to be a more obvious violation, as it forces a woman into an unnecessarily physically invasive and potentially painful examination. What is harder to comprehend is Sanger's insistence that any form of scanning is "physically and psychologically intrusive" because "it underscores for women that what they are about to do is wrong" (p. 126). If abortion is merely a medical procedure like any other, it is difficult to see why seeing the fetus constitutes "harassment masquerading as information" to Sanger (p. 127). If abortion is an act of killing—and this is hardly a controversial position any longer—then the viewing of an ultrasound scan merely confirms the obvious.

All in the Eye of the Beholder?

In fairness to Sanger, I can hardly fault her for the ludicrous material put out by some lone pro-life groups, such as the news release by the group Columbia Christians for Life in which they claimed that the satellite pictures of Hurricane Katrina looked like "a six-week unborn human child".[7] The idea was that this proved the hurricane to be divine retribution on America for abortion. As Sanger is kind enough to point out, "there are, of course, more scientific explanations about why disasters happen and why" (p. 70)—which is very helpful as pro-lifers are, by definition, flat-Earth-believing, tin-hat-wearing luddites who don't understand science at all. Where I do fault Sanger is in her use of a straw man argument, a trap into which no serious academic should fall. The use of a, frankly, off-the-wall news release by a fringe organization as the starting point for exploring the increasing significance of the unborn child in contemporary culture was too obviously an attempt to undermine the increasing awareness and importance of the unborn within society.

It is not just the legal requirement to offer an ultrasound scan to women that Sanger appears to find problematic: the increasing social awareness of the unborn is similarly beyond the pale. Sanger writes: "Many Americans have been socialized, or perhaps indoctrinated, into accepting fetal interests as part of what concerned citizens and legislators think about" (p. 72). Indoctrinated? Warnings to pregnant women not to drink alcohol, smoke, or take part in aggressive contact sports are a form of indoctrination? It may well be that in contemporary America, pregnant women are forced to stand in serried

---

[7] Quoted in Sanger, *About Abortion*, p. 70.

ranks chanting the rights of the unborn as part of their ante-natal care—as a foreigner I might well be missing something. More seriously, it is difficult to see how our increased understanding of prenatal development can be anything other than welcome in a society which claims to value scientific progress.

Sanger is very keen to suggest at different points in the book that pro-lifers are essentially reading too much into images such as hurricanes and ultrasounds, but is quick to fall into the same trap herself. Sanger gleefully recounts the disastrous campaign led by a group of Christian students who handed out tiny model babies to their fellow high-schoolers, who then proceeded to abuse the models, flush them down toilets, set them on fire, and turn their heads inside out to resemble rubber penises. Where most readers would see examples of puerile teenage behavior here, Sanger thought that "the conversion of fetuses to penises was distinctly transgressive, a sort of campy form of defiance" (p. 94). No—still seeing a group of teenage boys being gross.

Few of us would, I suspect, be gullible enough to believe the old adage that "the camera never lies." It is hardly a revelation to discover that photographic images can be manipulated, Photoshopped, and made to look markedly different to the person who originally stood in front of the camera. However, Sanger's obsession with trying to prove that ultrasound images are by definition manipulative constructs reads like a particularly persistent case of denial. Her deconstruction of the film *The Silent Scream* is a case in point. She quotes critics who describe the footage of an unborn baby being killed in an abortion as fusing "the anerotic sentimental structure of the infomercial and the docudrama with the pornotropic fantasies of a snuff film" (p. 83). The only way *The Silent Scream* may be compared with a snuff film is that it involves a vulnerable human being getting killed. I could not possibly gauge whether or not abortionists become sexually aroused whilst performing or filming abortions, but that is surely not the issue. *The Silent Scream* shows an unborn baby dying in an abortion. Whatever weird and wonderful ways abortion advocates respond to the film says nothing about the film itself, but the imputing of pornographic connotations to an abortion film may say a great deal more about the beholder than the beheld.

A half-truth Sanger is keen to exploit in her skilled dismissal of the obvious is the tendency of human beings to see human forms and faces everywhere—for example, seeing the Moon as a giant face, or seeing a humanoid figure in a cloud. However, the glaring difficulty about the unborn child is that it looks like exactly what it is. There is no need for "the desire to see a human form"; the human form is evidently there on the grainy ultrasound screen, wriggling, sucking its thumb, or having a snooze. It might be fairer to say that abortion advocates have conditioned themselves so thoroughly to see a blob of cells that they cannot bring themselves to see anything else.

False Comparisons

A tactic Sanger uses throughout the book to belittle the pro-life position is to create false comparisons, taking a contemporary image or debating point and comparing it with something regarded today as backward or ridiculous. Therefore, concerns over the existence of a visible embryonic tail in the early stages of development and the stir it caused in the 1920s around the time of the Scopes trial is effortlessly placed alongside awareness today of the fetal heartbeat and the symbolism of the "tiny feet" lapel pins popular among some pro-lifers.

A particularly bizarre comparison involves a grindingly long account of spiritualist photography in late Victorian times, where grief-stricken families would be made to believe that a photographer had captured the spirit of a dead relative. "A modern variation of spirit photography is the prenatal, sometimes preconception, visualization of children" (p. 145). In a word—no. Neither the fraudulent activities of Victorian charlatans nor the happy dreaming of what a future child might be like are anything like a picture of someone who is actually there. The comparison is pointless and absurd.

Teenagers going to court to request an abortion are talked about in the same chapter as "16th-century pardon seekers" (pp. 172–73). There is apparently a great deal of similarity between a minor requesting an abortion before a judge and a prisoner pleading with the king of France to be spared a very bloody execution. Apparently, there is also a comparison to be made between teenagers in court and the McCarthy hearings. I am amazed Sanger didn't squeeze in a reference to the Inquisition for good measure.

Elsewhere, some of Sanger's comparisons unwittingly play into her opponents' hands so catastrophically that if a pro-life advocate had made the comparison, they would be greeted with shrieks of faux outrage. Sanger sees similarities between a fetal scan which "exists in relation to the impending demise of the thing represented" (p. 131) and wartime photographs of people about to die, including prisoners of the Khmer Rouge: "Looking at these photos—some of prisoners with children—is always deeply distressing. One is aware of the impending loss even now. Ultrasound images are meant to create a visual

construction of loss for women awaiting an abortion"
(p. 131). Quite.

Post-Mortem Pregnancy

There are some areas about which Sanger is quite simply wrong, such as when discussing the rare situation
in which a pregnant woman is kept on life support to
try to save the baby. The very title "post-mortem pregnancy" shows a failure to understand what is medically
involved in such cases, as is her reference to the woman's
body in this case as a "corpse" (p. 202). This particular
issue is complex and very distressing, but a fundamental
point when a person is on life support is that they are not
dead. They may be being kept artificially alive, and the
means used may be unduly burdensome, but the patient
is not actually dead. Sanger betrays her own confusion by
describing a woman kept alive in such a way as becoming
"an incubator" (p. 204), but much as society tends to be
repulsed by the mistreatment of dead bodies, only the
living have rights. If the woman's rights were violated by
being kept on life support, she was by definition alive,
not dead.

When discussing cases involving men demanding the
destruction of IVF embryos, Sanger makes an unfounded
assumption about public opinion to reinforce her views
about the way women are judged. "Women who choose
abortion are selfish; men who destroy frozen embryos are
self-regarding" (p. 210). In reality, when Natallie Evans hit
the headlines in Britain after her failed legal battle to stop
her ex-fiancé from ordering the destruction of their IVF
embryos, the man was forced to acknowledge in a press
conference: "I can absolutely understand people saying

I've been heartless".[8] The media did not look entirely favourably towards the man who had human embryos destroyed in the face of tearful resistance from a woman rendered infertile by cancer treatment.

Nothing to Shout About

Sanger quite rightly points out at different stages of the book that women do not talk about their abortions, causing abortion to remain secret within many families. However, in seeking to define the difference between privacy and secrecy, she takes a wholly irresponsible position regarding abortions among minors. She cites attorney general Phil Kline's attempts to gain the medical records of underage girls who had obtained abortions, a case that collapsed because the legislature determined that "sexual activity of a minor did not in itself and without proof of harm constitute reportable child abuse" (p. 59). The widespread toleration and ignoring of underage sex by medical professionals, schools and the police is coming back to haunt the authorities in Britain in the wake of the inquiry into the Rotherham and Oxfordshire abuse scandals (for non-UK readers, a ring of paedophiles situated in Rotherham groomed and abused girls over a lengthy period of time under the noses of the authorities, helped by an underlying assumption that underage sex was acceptable and should not be queried).

Like many abortion apologists, Sanger is very keen on women talking about their abortions to "normalize" the process, imagining that this will bring abortion opponents

---

[8] "I Will Never Become a Mother", *Daily Mirror*, 11 April 2007, https://www.mirror.co.uk/news/uk-news/i-will-never-become-a-mother-465693.

round to the understanding that all kinds of women have abortions and abortion is therefore no big deal. She quotes the claim that people who oppose abortion are "much less likely than their pro-choice peers to hear abortion secrets and as such think they do not know any woman who has had one" (pp. 217–18). This is a common argument—pro-lifers think the way they do because they live in a bubble and have no idea the way the real world works. I wonder if Sanger has any idea of how many women actively involved in the pro-life movement have themselves had abortions. In my experience, being known as a pro-life campaigner makes a person a magnet for abortion stories, either from women determined to educate me into understanding that abortion really is absolutely fine or, more commonly, from women who need to talk to someone and tell "the secret". Talking about abortion apparently "reframes abortion's status from presumptive moral outrage to that of a simple medical procedure" (p. 230), but this is perhaps the most absurd generalization in a book replete with them. No one can predict how much talking about abortion is likely to influence the listener. I have known people break down talking about the moment their wife/mother/sister talked about her abortion, because they were made aware of lost offspring, a lost sibling or another lost relative.

More problematically for the pro-abortion side, the desperation to get women talking about their abortions very quickly turns nasty when women start talking about how much they regret their abortions. Talking about abortion is fine as long as women are good little girls and stick to the script. As soon as women start getting all negative about it, they are bullied, insulted, and have various syndromes attributed to them (but not postabortion syndrome, we don't talk about that either), and every possible attempt is made to shut them up.

Abortion and Miscarriage

Almost inevitably in a book about abortion, the discussion about miscarriage is depressingly insensitive and flawed. Miscarriage, readers are told, "appears natural, in contrast to abortion's deliberate quality, and miscarriage has a lack of materiality; some early miscarriages manifest as a heavy period" (pp. 84–85). Where to begin? Miscarriage does not "appear" natural; it is a naturally occurring event, however unintended and unwanted by the woman concerned. That is the reason it is different from abortion. Nor is it correct to say that miscarriage is not a political issue. The need for more research into the factors behind miscarriage and the treatment of women who miscarry are pertinent political issues for anyone concerned about women's health. The lack of "materiality" is another non sequitur. Depending upon the timing, miscarriage can be distressingly material with a woman left to deal, usually on her own, with a tiny body; but even when miscarriage is early enough to "manifest as a heavy period", it does not lessen the distressing reality for the woman that she has experienced a terrible loss. In my own experience, the absence of a palpable body following pregnancy loss only made the pain more difficult to bear because I had nothing, no proof whatsoever that I had ever been pregnant, beyond the excessive pain and bleeding, and the slow return of my body to its pre-pregnant state. Women who suffer miscarriage are almost as much of a nuisance to abortion advocates as women who regret their abortions, grieving mothers who draw the world's attention to the lost lives they mourn.

Important Points Raised

Unlike many abortion advocates, Sanger has the intellectual honesty to raise a number of pertinent points which others tend to avoid or dismiss out of hand. She admits that abortion can be painful for women: "For some women, abortion registers as a profound loss, the date or the projected birth date reflected upon, sometimes commemorated, for years to come" (p. ix). She also acknowledges the morally dubious issue of rape exceptions, which "produces a rather sharp inequality among fetuses" (p. 11). Sanger draws attention to the terrifying collusion of millions in the abortion industry—though she would not see this as problematic: "If each of the 700,000 or so women and girls who terminated a pregnancy in 2015 interacted with only a few others along the way—one nurse, one partner, one pastor, one babysitter for the kids, one good friend, one receptionist—several million more people are involved" (p. x). When individuals dismiss antiabortion arguments with the old cliché "If you don't like abortion, you don't have to have one", it is worth remembering that when abortions are carried out on a massive scale within society, few individuals avoid any direct or indirect responsibility.

Dubious Conclusions

Sanger concludes her book with a reflection that reveals how out-of-touch abortion advocates are with social trends. "As abortion becomes less stigmatized," she muses, "as it will in time, it will come to be regarded like other medical decisions—thoughtfully taken and exercised without a gauntlet of picketers on the pavement or hard looks at home" (p. 238). I cannot vouch for how hard anyone will be looked at in the future, but if surveys are anything to go by—not to mention the rise in the number of young people involved with pro-life advocacy—Sanger's prediction may be very far from the mark.

APPENDIX 2

A Moral Case for Abortion?*

The recent book The Moral Case for Abortion *by Ann Furedi, a prominent UK abortion provider, fails to engage the positions of her opponents while rehashing the well-worn "my body, my choice" argument.*[†]

In Britain, Ann Furedi's name is synonymous with abortion apologetics. She is the director of one of Britain's largest chains of abortion facilities, and she makes frequent appearances at debates and in the press, defending abortion with a zeal that would be regarded as fundamentalist if she were a member of a religious sect. Furedi is a proud former member of the (defunct) Revolutionary Communist Party (which really was as barking mad as it sounds) and contributor to *Living Marxism* (alas, no longer living), and now writes for its successor *Spiked Online.* Over the years, she has picked some bizarre targets for her ire, including the parents of children murdered during

---

[*] The following originally appeared in Fiorella Nash, "A Moral Case for Abortion?", *Catholic World Report*, 18 November 2016, www.catholicworld report.com/2016/11/18/a-moral-case-for-abortion/.

[†] Ann Furedi, *The Moral Case for Abortion* (London: Palgrave Macmillan, 2016).

the Dunblane shooting[1] (how dare they be permitted to express opinions on prime-time TV and be taken seriously?) and organizations attempting to protect children from peer abuse (yes, Ms Furedi, children do sometimes get sexually abused by other minors).

It's fair to say, therefore, that a woman who has been known to dismiss her opponents as "vile scum"[2] and who trivialized Kermit Gosnell's house of horrors as "pretty shoddy service"[3] was going to have to work fairly hard to be taken seriously by me, but I genuinely expected a book published by Palgrave Macmillan to have some substance— even substance with which I was likely to disagree.

Instead, the reader is treated to a well-worn expansion of the "my body, my choice, me, me, me" argument, and the whole book reads like an affirmation of abortion by pro-aborts for pro-aborts. For all its intellectual posturing, at no point is there any real attempt at facing the arguments against abortion in any depth; the pro-life side is just assumed to be wrong and any right-minded person ought to understand this without being told, whilst those who oppose abortion are portrayed as representing a tiny and therefore fairly irrelevant minority (so irrelevant in fact that Ms Furedi has dedicated an entire book and a substantial part of her career to refuting the pro-life position).

Furedi's style itself is at times highly engaging and articulate, for all its odd quirks, such as her cloyingly deferential

---

[1] On 13 March 1996, a gunman walked into a primary school in the Scottish town of Dunblane, killing sixteen young children and their teacher and injuring over thirty others before committing suicide. It remains the only instance of a school shooting in the UK and caused widespread shock.

[2] "Pro-life Anger at 'Scum' Slur", BBC News, 30 May 2001, http://news .bbc.co.uk/news/vote2001/hi/english/wales/newsid_1360000/1360467.

[3] "USA: Doctor Charged with Illegal Abortions", *Abortion Review*, 25 January 2011, http://www.reproductivereview.org/index.php/site/article/910/.

tone towards thinkers she admires. She repeatedly adds the adverb "wisely" when introducing a quote from someone who backs up her argument, a habit I have noted in her other writings. The central problem, besides the poor arguments, is that there is so little substance to the style. For example, she speaks warmly of the "Hippocratic tradition" whilst failing somehow to note that this splendid tradition involved an equally splendid oath which prohibits doctors from abortion. It is hard to imagine that the Hippocratic tradition counts for very much to the director of an organization whose doctors break the oath every day of their lives.

It is also difficult to know where to start on such a flawed treatment of abortion, but a number of key issues bear closer inspection, if nothing else because they are so central to the current pro-abortion position.

Conscience

The importance of conscience looms large at various points in the book. Having spent much of my youth campaigning to free prisoners of conscience, I am never very impressed by anyone who seems to think that "conscience" is synonymous with "I'll do whatever makes my life most comfortable and I will feel very righteous about doing so"; but Furedi is at her most bewildering when considering the importance of conscience. She is very, very keen on freedom of conscience when it comes to a woman having an abortion. Freedom of conscience in this context is inviolable; it is practically what makes us human—unless of course you happen to be a member of the medical profession when the value of freedom of conscience mysteriously evaporates. Doctors who obey their conscience and refuse to perform abortions are "inevitably an impediment to good quality care".[4] Furedi then goes on cynically to undermine the motives of medics who express a conscientious objection; it is simply "a means to undermine the framework of abortion services".[5] Worse than that, it's really a form of laziness: "There is also a deep suspicion that, when medical students and trainees are under pressure, 'conscientious objection' becomes less an expression of faith and more an expression of a desire to cut down on their workload, or involvement in what they see as an unpleasant task".[6] Nothing judgmental there at all.

Furedi concedes that forcing doctors to perform abortion is not "practical or desirable", though the author apparently had no problem with the persecution of two Scottish Catholic midwives for refusing to supervise abortions at a Glasgow hospital. Indeed, so keen was she to ensure that the two women were prevented from exercising their choice not to be involved with abortion that Furedi's organization, the British Pregnancy Advisory Service (BPAS), directly intervened in the case and welcomed the court ruling against them. Furedi has a more magnanimous long-term plan to ensure that every future doctor is happy to do the abortion industry's dirty work: "The answer to the problems caused by the extent of conscientious objection is to work to convert clinicians to a different moral standpoint: one that does not regard abortion as a moral wrong, but sees it as an enabling act of consideration and faith in women's judgement over their own lives."[7] Indeed. Pregnant women can be trusted to

[4] Ann Furedi, *The Moral Case for Abortion* (London: Palgrave Macmillan, 2016), Kindle edition, chap. 6, doi: 2137. Subsequent quotations from this work will be cited by chapter number and doi number.
[5] Ibid., chap. 6, doi: 2128.
[6] Ibid., chap. 6, doi: 2137.
[7] Ibid., chap. 6, doi: 2156.

make their own decisions based on their personal values, but these heretical pro-life doctors must be converted to uphold the *correct* values and beliefs.

Misinformation

The book is replete with very basic errors. The terms "embryo" and "fetus" are used interchangeably as though the author is seriously unaware that they mean different things and that most women do not even know they are pregnant when their children are at the embryonic stage. She attempts on more than one occasion to conflate abortion and miscarriage: "in effect, the abortion pill causes a miscarriage much the same as the loss through 'natural' spontaneous miscarriages experienced by millions of women around the world".[8] Comparing the two experiences is wrong on so many levels, but using miscarriage as some kind of justification for abortion is hurtful to those very millions of women who go through the misery of losing a baby. It is also blatantly illogical. Millions die of disease every year, but this sad reality would hardly justify rounding up and hanging the same number of individuals.

It is also safe to say that Furedi could use a few history lessons. When discussing characters such as Marie Stopes, she laments: "It is ironic that the early 20th-century birth-control pioneers, Marie Stopes (in the UK) and Margaret Sanger (in the USA) are derided by today's opponents of abortion."[9] I suppose it is possible that a former member of the Revolutionary Communist Party really cannot see why opponents of abortion object to a woman who

[8] Ibid., chap. 4, doi: 1175.
[9] Ibid., chap. 4, doi: 1157.

sent racist love poems to Adolf Hitler[10] and peddled dangerous and unsanitary devices among poor women.[11] But then, Furedi seems equally unaware of the euphemism and gentle massaging of the facts about abortion put out by today's abortion industry—odd when she is one of its leading figures. "Modern medicine," she reassures us, "is built upon the principles of informed consent".[12] It is in doctors' interests to tell women the whole truth about what abortion involves—apparently. My own children have been directed (by a charity invited into their school) to information about abortion that describes chemical abortion as being "like a heavy period". By no stretch of the imagination is informed consent a given when it comes to abortion.

Then there are the glaring generalizations. "From the outset," we are confidently told, "autonomy was contested by religious leaders, traditional conservatives, and others who were distrustful of people making decisions for themselves."[13] Which leaders? And what particular outset are we talking about here? The Caveman Committee for the Suppression of Choice?

Those Horrid Pro-Lifers

Caricatures and criticisms of the pro-life movement are scattered throughout the book. Opponents of abortion are

---

[10] See Palash Ghosh, "Marie Stopes: Women's Rights Activist or Nazi Eugenicist?", *International Business Times*, 18 October 2012, http://www.ibtimes.com/marie-stopes-womens-rights-activist-or-nazi-eugenicist-848457.

[11] For further information on the early promotion of contraception, see Ann Farmer, *Prophets and Priests: The Hidden Face of the Birth Control Movement* (London: Saint Austin Press, 2002).

[12] Furedi, *Moral Case for Abortion*, chap. 3, doi: 917.

[13] Ibid., chap. 7, doi: 2341.

"fundamentalists". "Abortion's opponents have a tunnel vision focused only on the fetus."[14] Hmm. I can safely say that never in my entire life have I met a pro-life campaigner whose view was, "Sod the woman, the baby's all that matters." The opposite tends to be true. Whereas women who suffer after abortion tend to be written off as cranks or attention-seekers by abortion supporters, the groups that care for postabortive women were largely established by women who regretted their abortions and turned to the pro-life movement as the only place where they could receive compassionate help. Likewise, pro-life medical associations such as MaterCare International work tirelessly to save and improve the lives of both pregnant mothers and their babies in countries where maternal mortality is still shamefully high.

However, Furedi also informs us that "very few opponents of abortion are able to claim that they oppose it under any circumstance".[15] This is news to me since virtually all pro-life groups hold this line, but then, pro-life campaigners are merely "a small but loud minority of those who are fundamentally against reproductive choice for reasons based on faith and doctrine".[16] Not long afterwards, she concedes that the religious label she has just imposed is in fact a myth, and that opposition to abortion represents a broad camp.

For US readers who may be unaware of this point, Furedi is a great champion of freedom of speech, freedom of conscience and all manner of civil liberties (including the right to produce and consume pornography)—except in the immediate vicinity of abortion facilities, where she

[14] Ibid., chap. 3, doi: 726.
[15] Ibid., chap. 3, doi: 660.
[16] Ibid., chap. 1, doi: 173.

is making aggressive attempts to ban individuals from exercising their freedom to pray, protest and engage women in conversation. Like Furedi, I am not a fan of the indiscriminate use of graphic imagery (possibly as a result of having a picture of a dismembered baby thrust in my face shortly after I had suffered a miscarriage), but can she really be serious in her belief that such images are pornographic or are used with the express purpose of doing harm? She writes: "Of course, the primary concern is the woman, but for many women and their doctors, the fetus seems to matter too. This is why the pictures of dismembered fetuses from later abortions are so cruel; they don't inform women, but taunt them".[17] Not so. They are cruel because they reveal a cruel procedure, and shooting the messenger is not going to change that. But apparently: "This reveling in the gore, broken bodies, severed limbs, and crushed heads has a pornographic quality".[18] Presumably the same could be said of any human rights organization which uses photographic evidence, as so many now do. The hideous photographs of torture paraded by the Falun Gong outside the Chinese embassy offend my senses, they leave me feeling physically unwell and I worry about children seeing them in such a public place, but are the Falun Gong really *pornographers* for wanting the world to see what is happening to their co-religionists?

The Idolatry of Choice

The sanctity of choice is vaunted throughout the book, with John Stuart Mill making a cameo appearance. The

---

[17] Ibid., chap. 5, doi: 1558.
[18] Ibid., chap. 3, doi: 796.

"choice" mantra has always been dangerously nonsensical and for very sound reasons. The freedom to make choices about one's life is highly important to who we are and our place in society, but choices are not made in a vacuum. To claim that pro-aborts are right to call themselves pro-choice because "the outcome of the decision is irrelevant to pro-choice advocates" and because "life is full of decisions, and it is who makes them that matters",[19] makes little logical or moral sense. The decision matters. Each and every choice we make has a definite purpose and must be judged—and if necessary impeded—based on the merits of that choice and its intended outcome. I do not expect a man's decision to mug an old lady to be celebrated (or even permitted) in the same way as his choice to assist her in crossing a busy road.

That is the nettle never grasped, either in the book or in the wider abortion discourse. Choice is paraded without any acknowledgement of the fact that we limit choice in all sorts of areas all the time, preventing individuals from making certain decisions and punishing them if they do (I might be quite keen to thump my manager at this precise moment but would rather not be arraigned for assault), and only a fully fledged anarchist truly desires the wholesale breakdown in the rule of law. Upholding reasonable laws that check our behavior need not "stunt and constrain" anyone.

The "Special" Child

Furedi should be credited with having moved on a little in her understanding of disability from the days she argued

[19] Ibid., chap. 7, doi: 2536.

that a woman should be supported in aborting a baby with a disability that she might "dread" and "wish dead",[20] as though she were giving birth to some kind of monster. But Furedi has simply exchanged one ignorant and judgmental assumption about the horrors of disability with a more patronizing one. "A diagnosis of Down's syndrome may compel one woman to end her pregnancy, while another decides to embrace the child as 'special'."[21] The term Special (no inverted commas necessary) is merely shorthand for Special Educational Needs, not the sentimental epithet Furedi implies. Whilst I cannot speak for the parents of children with Down's syndrome, I can say with complete sincerity that I do not embrace my autistic son as "special"; I embrace him as a human being with the right to life. Women do not generally love and accept their disabled children because they think that they are little angels gift-wrapped by Jesus to enlighten them: my son is my son who happens to have a disabling condition. He is no more or less "special" than his other siblings; it does not take any more effort to love him or accept him than the others—if anything, the opposite is true. First and foremost, he is my son; but love seems to be the one quality abortion advocates find hardest to get their autonomous heads around.

Are We Talking about Human Life Here?
Yes but No but Yes but No but YES

Perhaps most predictably of all within the context of the abortion debate, it is the status of the unborn with which

[20] Ann Furedi, "Hard Choices: How We Can—and Should—Explore Ethical Concerns about Abortion while Remaining Committed to Women's Needs", *Catholics for Choice Magazine*, Autumn 1999, http://www.catholics forchoice.org/issues_publications/hard-choices/.

[21] Furedi, *Moral Case for Abortion*, chap. 7, doi: 2537.

the author struggles and fails to come up with a coherent or humane answer. It is in part simply that the science does not offer much consolation for those who wish to deny the humanity of the unborn (or embryo or fetus or whatever the preferred term), and Furedi is forced to acknowledge repeatedly, "Yes, abortion involves a 'killing' in the sense that it stops a beating heart, but not in the sense that it stops a person from living."[22] Unable to avoid the trumpeting elephant in the room whenever the morality of abortion is discussed, the author lapses into bizarre judgments about the value of life and which lives matter enough to be protected, a dark road most of us would rather not go down, knowing inevitably where such dehumanizing judgments about the value of particular sections of society can lead.

Pesky pro-lifers, who are inconvenient enough to have science on their side, are dismissed for apparently being too scientific. "Could there be a more empty and degraded sense of humanity than to reduce it to its biological components, when human life is truly so much more?"[23] Well, possibly the empty and degraded sense of humanity that allows a member of the medical profession to inject an unborn baby's heart with poison or remove a tiny human being from the womb limb by limb. Possibly. In no other area of social justice are groups which fight for the rights of specific groups accused of "reducing" human life "to its biological components" simply for reminding the world that we are undeniably talking about human lives.

Furedi's arguments against comparisons with genocides such as the Holocaust come across as particularly heartless. She writes: "The qualities that the embryo lacks are precisely those that make the terror of extermination so dreadful for individual people: the capacity for

22 Ibid., chap. 8, doi: 2674–79.
23 Ibid., chap. 5, doi: 1597–602.

self-consciousness, the capacity for rational thought, the capacity to imagine a future for oneself, the capacity to remember a past involving oneself and the capacity for being a subject of non-momentary interests."[24]

Is that so? If (God forbid) a gunman burst into my house with a machine gun blazing, it is likely that I would have enough time to die frightened and distraught, whereas my toddler would have no capacity to understand that she was about to be murdered. In what way would her killing be more morally acceptable than mine? How would her lack of awareness make her murder less of a tragedy, less of an outrage? Whereas I have some sympathy with Furedi's disdain for using past atrocities as a point of comparison for abortion (though Furedi is perfectly happy to compare the prohibition of abortion with slavery—some atrocities are evidently not off-limits), her argument falls down over her own poor grasp of why genocide is such a terrible crime against humanity. Like my toddler, the millions of young children and infants who have been killed as part of genocidal atrocities over the centuries can have had little or no "capacity to remember a past involving oneself". No one with an ounce of humanity would suggest that the youngest human lives lost to violence do not matter. If anything, we feel an even greater sense of horror at the thought of little ones being slaughtered along with their parents.

Furedi writes, "Essentially the point for us is not when life begins, but *when life begins to matter.*"[25] Furedi makes some interesting pronouncements on that issue. "It is indeed this absence of 'fully-humanness' that allows some of us to dismiss any claim to 'the right to life of the

[24] Ibid., chap. 8, doi: 2685–90.
[25] Ibid., chap. 5, doi: 1797; emphasis in the original.

unborn child'."[26] We are also informed: "Our life story is not written by God, or by nature, but in a great part by ourselves—through the decisions we make. The fetus possesses the life the Greeks called *zoe*—which is common to every being that possesses a beating heart and its own DNA (be it a cat, snake, or horse)—but it has no *bios*; and it is bios that puts the 'human' in human life."[27] Wrong on so many levels, it's difficult to know where to start other than to state the obvious: *Who should have the power to decide when and which human life matters enough to save?* And if a fetus does not possess "bios", it is safe to say that a newborn and even a toddler lacks precisely that quality. By the same argument, any child below the age of reason could fall into the category of not really mattering; an elderly person with dementia, a car-crash victim in a coma—the examples are endless, well-known and completely ignored here.

Children as Property

Few people today, I suspect, would assert that children are the property of their parents in the same way that an adult might own a bookcase or a potted plant; and it would certainly ring alarm bells with child protection services if a mother screamed at a social worker: "That child is mine! She's my property and I'll sell her to the mafia if I want to! I bore her; I am her sole care-giver—stop interfering with my conscience!" But it is precisely this incredibly anachronistic belief that parents own their children and have absolute rights over them that Furedi upholds in her defense of abortion. "The contents of her womb are hers

---

[26] Ibid., chap. 5, doi: 1705.
[27] Ibid., chap. 5, doi: 1753–58.

and hers alone, by virtue of their location in her womb. How she values the embryo or fetus that she carries inside her body is for her to decide."[28] Geography is not and has never been an adequate defense of extermination—a baby is no more "the contents of the uterus" than my children are the contents of my house. Clearly the fact that the baby develops inside the body of a woman is highly significant and must always be taken into account within both the abortion debate and with regard to the treatment of pregnant women by society,[29] but the baby's absolute state of dependency does not end with birth, and few advocate the "termination" of newborns.

Various attempts through inadequate analogies are used to defend a mother's right to refuse to sustain her own unborn baby, but Furedi's comparison with a mother refusing to donate a kidney is particularly unconvincing. Besides the fact that it would be a pretty mean-spirited parent who would refuse a kidney donation to her own child, transplant may well constitute extraordinary means, whereas pregnancy can hardly be regarded as such. Abortion is a violent assault upon a human life, not a refusal to sustain it. Even if any of these arguments in terms of rights and ownership held as much water as abortion advocates like to believe, I found myself turning the pages of the book with the same persistent questions going around my head: Where does love come into all of this? What about

[28] Ibid., chap. 8, doi: 2656.

[29] For an in-depth analysis of the symbiotic relationship between mother and baby, see Dr Helen Watt's scholarly work *The Ethics of Pregnancy, Abortion and Childbirth: Exploring Moral Choices in Childbearing (Routledge Annals of Bioethics)* (New York: Routledge, 2016). For my review of her book, see "New Book by UK Ethicist Takes Long, Hard Look at Pregnancy and Its Meaning", *Catholic World Report*, 22 July 2016, http://www.catholicworld report.com/2016/07/22/new-book-by-uk-ethicist-takes-long-hard-look-at -pregnancy-and-its-meaning/.

decency? Humanity? Dare I use the word "virtue"? Does anyone really want to live in a society where the lives of the most innocent are regarded as cannon fodder in the battle for autonomy? Is that *enlightenment* in any sense of the word?

The reader is assured by Furedi that "there is a strong and compelling case for a woman to make her own choices about the future of her pregnancy—and for abortion— if that is her choice."[30] But if there is such a case, it is not to be found among the pages of this book, for all the soundbites. "The freedom to make moral choices is the most important freedom we have; the freedom to act on our moral choices is the most important privilege we can claim."[31] Splendid, I am now going to exercise my moral choice to drive off in my car without fastening my safety belt because I deem myself not to need it and only I will get killed if I get hurtled through the windshield during a crash. The choice to smash myself up is mine and mine alone; it is my body after all, and the state has no right to dictate. While I'm at it, I will drive above the patriarchal speed limit since I, in good conscience, can see no reason to stick to some arbitrary rule invented by men to control me and make me late for the school run. As for the safety of the other occupants of my vehicle—my car, my choice, my right to decide. The contents of my vehicle are mine and mine alone.

To make my reading experience complete, Furedi cannot resist leveling a criticism at women like me who identify as both pro-life and feminist, written with the tone of a disappointed schoolmistress: "It is unfortunate that, in denying the importance of individual autonomy, certain

---

[30] Furedi, *Moral Case for Abortion*, chap. 8, doi: 2641–48.
[31] Ibid., chap. 8, doi: 2739.

strands of feminism have taken positioned themselves [sic] in opposition to the just fight for choice."[32] No, Ann, naughty little pro-life feminists like me are not opposed to a just fight. We are fighting one. A fight for the right to life, without which all your eloquent utterances about choice and autonomy are meaningless.

[32] Ibid., chap. 7, doi: 2546.